Is This Guidebook Right for You?

Have you ever had any of these thoughts:

- How much ceremony is too much ceremony? When is ceremony not the best next step?
- If your shaman is not from your culture or local to you, what can you do to integrate after a ceremony? Who do you turn to?
- What do you do when ceremony reveals trauma?
- What kind of support do you need post-ceremony to help yourself fully heal?
- How can you live in deeper harmony with visionary plant medicine?
- How can you ground your work with visionary plants and walk the teachings in your daily life?

After the Ceremony Ends helps you understand how you can embrace your work with visionary plants much more fully so that you can heal more profoundly and grow from the place of your deepest authenticity.

The ceremony is only the beginning: Integrating your experiences is **critical** to your transformation and, without it, you risk becoming more fractured and destabilized. Learn how to work with visionary plants more consciously to find the wholeness and freedom that you seek!

An insightful and comprehensive guide that assists explorers on the visionary plant medicine path to better understand and integrate the complexities of their journeys and move forward with greater clarity and wisdom. Highly recommended.

Shonagh Home, Shamanic
Therapist, Author and Poet

A ubiquitous hunger for wholeness, purpose and meaning is accelerating the demand for Plant Spirit Medicines around the world. But the same conditions that drive this hunger mean most Westerners are ill equipped to manage and integrate the peak experiences occasioned by these powerful substances. Coder's guidebook provides a welcomed anecdote to the common misconception that Plant Spirit Medicines are a shortcut to healing. Through careful study and personal experience, she skillfully impresses upon us that deep and sustainable emotional healing is a process requiring courage, fortitude, and most of all effort. This practical guidebook is a must read for those considering or currently using Plant Spirit Medicine in their healing journeys.

Dr. Gerald Thomas, Collaborating Scientist,
Centre for Addiction Research of BC

*Such aids to perception are medicine not diets, and...
the use of a medicine should lead to a more healthful
mode of living.*

—Alan Watts

Casa de Raices y Alas Books

Boulder, Colorado

Copyright © 2017 by Katherine E. Coder

All rights reserved. This book or any portion thereof may not be reproduced or used in any manner whatsoever without the express written permission of the publisher except for the use of brief quotations in a book review.

Printed in the United States of America

First Printing, 2017

ISBN 978-0-9988379-0-1

Casa de Raices y Alas Books

2571 Mapleton Avenue

Boulder, CO 80304

www.katherinecoder.com

CONTENTS

Preface vii
Acknowledgements xv
Chapter 1: Introducing Visionary Plant Medicine Integration: Power and Pitfalls 1
Chapter 2: Expert Guidance 27
Chapter 3: Trauma Release 35
Chapter 4: Psychospiritual Discipline and Practices 45
Chapter 5: Reflection, Inner Listening, and Creative Expression 51
Chapter 6: Meaning Making 57
Chapter 7: Spaciousness and Time 63
Chapter 8: Nature and Grounding 67
Chapter 9: Adequate Physical Care 75
Chapter 10: Cultivating Virtues 81
Chapter 11: Turning Outward: The Return to the World 85
Appendix: Theoretical Basis and Scientific Support for Visionary Plant Medicine Integration 91
References 99
Recommended Reading 111
About the Author 113

PREFACE

Spirit will initiate you through the doorway of Challenge—as you meet those challenges, they weather you, deepen you, and test your integrity. It's like when a potter puts a pot inside a kiln. They heat it up for a while and pull it out and then heat it up again. It's got to be just right or it will crack and won't hold what it was made for. When someone reaches a level of spiritual integrity where they can hold what's being poured into them by Spirit, they operate differently.

—Anonymous

Look deep into nature and you will understand everything better.

—Albert Einstein

WHAT IS VISIONARY PLANT MEDICINE INTEGRATION?

Visionary Plant Medicine Integration is the process by which a visionary plant medicine practitioner is transformed by the teachings, visions, and experiences from visionary plant medicine and incorporates those changes into daily life. Visionary plant medicine integration can often necessitate attending to traumas to release them fully; understanding the manifestations of ego in one's daily experience; and, practicing new ways of thinking, conceptualizing, and being that are in alignment with wisdom teachings.

Visionary plant medicine integration, in this definition, explores the use of visionary plant medicines, which are plants that induce visionary states that are used in service of health and healing for individuals and communities. Examples of popular visionary plant medicines in the West today include iboga, psilocybin mushrooms, ayahuasca, huachuma (San Pedro), salvia divinorum, and peyote. Visionary plant medicines have been used in sacred contexts by aboriginal peoples for thousands of years, and our human ancestors from around the globe can often point to visionary plant medicines that were used to connect to the divine (McKenna, 1992; Sayin, 2014).

This guidebook is primarily focused on the use of such plants in ceremonial and otherwise sacred contexts where the intention of the facilitator is to guide the participant or participants in a ritual to assist them in their growth towards wholeness. These sacred rituals can also be facilitated to help a group or community heal as a collective. Visionary plant medicines can also be worked with alone in a sacred context if the practitioner is capable of providing their own container for their work. To be transparent,

I am biased against the solitary use of such plants as I do not believe most practitioners to be capable of providing adequate containment and protection for themselves, unless they have had a significant amount of experience (years) working with such plants under the guidance of a master teacher. If ceremonial experiences are not guarded and attended to adequately by expert space holders, the visionary experience has a greater possibility of causing psychic harm, which can cause persistent difficulties for the visionary plant medicine practitioner well beyond the ceremony.

This guidebook is less focused on the use of synthetic hallucinogens such as LSD and MDMA. It is also not focused on the recreational use of synthetic or plant-based vision-inducing substances. Having said this, the guidance provided in this manual can certainly be applied to synthetic substances if the practitioner desires such. In my personal experience, recreational use of visionary synthetic and plant-based substances does not necessarily include an intention to heal or become whole. Often recreational experience is just that – recreation intended for fun, entertainment, and the like. When a recreational experience deviates into one that brings the user into a space of healing, the guidance provided here can certainly be of value if the user desires.

WHY I OFFER GUIDANCE IN VISIONARY PLANT MEDICINE INTEGRATION

My doctoral work in transpersonal psychology, combined with four years of personal work with visionary plant medicine, entheogens, as well as my work as a facilitator of visionary plant medicine ceremony has led me to understand the profound importance of integrating the visionary plant medicine teachings.

What I often see, and what I experienced personally, was a tendency to participate in another ceremony instead of integrating the previous ceremony. No one guided me towards integration in my work with visionary plant medicine, including the various shamans I worked with from Colombia, Peru, Ecuador, Gabon, Puerto Rico, and the United States.

The answer was always more ceremony.

After many ceremonies with minimal integration, I began to notice that further ceremonial work was not helping me. I also noticed that my physical body was suffering from the intensity of the medicines and the frequency with which I was working with them. At one point, I became so depleted that I knew I had the choice between going to the hospital and taking an extended break.

I have spent the last two years integrating my extensive experiences with visionary plant medicine, finally allowing my system to take in the numerous teachings I received. Some of the teachings are so profound that I will spend the rest of my life integrating them. With the integration, I am coming into wholeness, releasing that which is not serving me, deepening in my contemplative practice and self-healing work, and allowing myself to embody more each day from what I experienced.

One of my challenges in getting the support that I needed was the reality of what I'm calling "missionary medicine" and what others have referred to as a "missionary enterprise" (Saez, 2012, p. xxiii). Hardly any of the shamans/medicine people I worked with lived locally. And, often they did not speak English, my native language. There was no way to ask many of these medicine people for help integrating as they moved from one place to another, never staying in any one place too long. By default, I was left to care for myself with the comforting but unprofessional assistance of my visionary plant medicine tribe.

As that kind of support was not sufficient, I sought out professional help for psychotherapy, energy medicine, nutrition, bodywork, acupuncture, and other various healing modalities to support my integration process. Time in nature, grounding practices, meditation/prayer, journaling, exercise, reading, and with trusted friends and companions on the path all helped me integrate my experiences and begin to "walk the talk."

I come at writing this integration guide both as a student and a teacher. I have shared my role as a student in sharing a bit of my journey above. All of the recommendations I am making for integration come from my own personal experiences. And, I draw on my training as a transpersonal psychologist and my work with clients to help inform the theoretical underpinnings of visionary plant medicine integration as well as the maxims for deep processes of integration. Many of my clients work with visionary plant medicines as part of their healing journey so I have been gifted with the opportunity to serve as a guide in their paths. One of my favorite co-therapists is ayahuasca. "She" tends to point out and reveal some highly critical psychodynamics!

If I had to share a few words about my viewpoint of psychology and spirituality, I would have to look to these few sentences by Neal Goldsmith (2007):

> *With the exception of biologically based illness, psychology must come to be seen as the science of spiritual maturity. We call people "neurotic," when in reality, it is not a medical illness they are suffering from, but spiritual immaturity. We must redefine spirituality, too, not as supernatural, but simply as the natural unfolding of the wise, mature end of the normative template for human developmental psychology. From this perspective, then, "healing" can take place only when we get beneath our modern imago to rest at the ground of our being and so to naturally unfold according to our perfect, internal template for development. (p. 125)*

This guide is not written as an exhaustive guide to integration complete with an abundance of research-based and theoretical support for the topics within. I am balancing a few objectives: I want to provide empirically-based support, anecdotal evidence and examples, and personal notes when it seems helpful. I wanted to create a guide that is more complete and accessible than what currently exists, and one that is accessible to the average, non-scholarly, reader while still retaining a richness of content. I am hoping this can be a guide you can read in an hour or two, take with you on your journey to the Amazon, or pass along to a friend.

I also must note that this guidebook is not geared as an advertisement for visionary plant medicine replete with success stories of miraculous healings. As far as I can tell, there is plenty of that sort of thing out there. If anything, this guidebook is written as a counterpoint to that type of information. This guidebook is written to awaken your consciousness to a complete understanding of this type of healing work – which includes the shadow elements as well as the possibilities for profound healing which is often only available through integration. While spontaneous healings do happen with the plants and otherwise through other life experiences, my firm understanding is that those spontaneous healings are quite rare. What is more likely with visionary plant medicine use is a raising of consciousness and awareness that helps you see (your) life more fully, from a different perspective, and that gives you direction for where to seek your healing.

Wishing you many blessings of healing on your profound journey to live as your most essential self!

ACKNOWLEDGEMENTS

When I think of how many people I'd like to thank for their contribution to this guidebook, my mind swims with luminaries. This guidebook could not have been written without all of the mentors and professors I had at the Institute of Transpersonal Psychology who guided me in my studies of holistic forms of psychotherapeutic healing and philosophy. I'd like to thank my clinical mentors and supervisors as well as colleagues who taught me about the dynamics of healing and becoming whole. I'd also like to thank my spiritual teachers and mentors, notably Saniel Bonder and Linda Groves-Bonder, Michael Goodman, Malidoma Patrice Some, and Kane Tuma as well as my plant mentors *los ninos*, ayahuasca, San Pedro, and iboga for all of their guidance, healing, and support. Thank you to the shamans and medicine workers for holding sacred space and for teaching me about integrity in the shamanic process.

I'd like to thank Albert Garcia-Romeu, Gerald Thomas, Shonagh Home, and Hector Batiz for reading and offering edits for the manuscript. An author can get so lost in her thoughts writing in a vacuum! Your expertise, feedback, and comments were of tremendous help in finalizing this work. Thank you for your honorable work in the visionary plant medicine healing space!

Thank you to my dear soul friends who have been with me in the visionary plant medicine healing container and who have spent hours upon hours processing the many journeys into the visionary world.

Thank you to my clients who have taught me so much about what integration means from their unique intrapersonal landscapes and who helped me refine my own understanding of integration from the visionary plant medicine space.

And, thank you finally to our Earth Mother for holding the manifest space for all of my own healing to occur and for being such an integral aspect of my movement towards grounded presence.

CHAPTER 1

INTRODUCING VISIONARY PLANT MEDICINE INTEGRATION: POWER AND PITFALLS

Is there, in short, a medicine which can give us temporarily the sensation of being integrated, of being fully one with ourselves and with nature?... If so, the experience might offer clues to whatever else must be done to bring about full and continuous integration. It might be at least the tip of Ariadne's thread to lead us out of the maze in which all of us are lost from our infancy.

—Alan Watts

Many of us are turning to visionary plant medicine as a way to deeply heal and to spiritually awaken. Those who seek visionary plant medicine range from people who have worked for years in other therapeutic modalities to reach deep wounds to people who feel their own potential for consciousness and who want to explore that more fully.

A common misconception is that the visionary plants themselves will basically do the "heavy lifting" for you. What I mean by this is that people new to visionary plant medicine can often believe that the visionary plants themselves will completely heal them without any personal effort on their part other than ceremony attendance.

While visionary plant medicine practitioners can often feel a sense of energetic clearing after a ceremony that can ground them into an often wider perspective on reality, what I have seen is that the most significant teachings (or visions) the plants bring serve primarily to awaken your consciousness to key aspects of your personality and history that are creating misalignment for you. These teachings often show you the places in your psyche that need attention and healing. The visionary plant medicine work can also help you re-experience previously undigested psychic material so that it can be cleared from your unconscious and/or subconscious. This process of integrating previously marooned psychic experience is often felt as deeply freeing.

The visions of the plants can also awaken you to the profound fundamental non-separateness of life and existence. With these visions, practitioners can see their sense of separateness in the context of larger ultimate truth.

Whether it be healing or awakening or both, what is revealed may take a lifetime to fully integrate.

As Stolaroff (1993) writes

The role of psychedelics is often misunderstood. Many feel that having had wonderful experiences, they now have the answers and are somehow changed. And no doubt in many respects they are. But users often overlook the fact that there are usually heavy walls of conditioning and ignorance separating the surface mind from the core of our being. It is a blessing that psychedelics can set aside these barriers and give access to our real Self. But unless one is committed to the changes indicated, old habits of personality can rapidly reestablish themselves.

At this point many feel that repeating the experience will maintain the exalted state. It may, but most often change requires hard work and dedicated effort. Unfortunately this is not always clear during the experience itself; it has merely pointed the way and shown what is possible. If we like what we see, it is now up to us to bring about the changes indicated.

There is a grace period following profound psychedelic experiences when changes can rapidly be made. At this time one is infused with the power and wonder of new information. Moreover – and this is an area where valuable research can be done – the drug experience releases a great deal of bodily and psychic armoring that is tied to our neuroses.

> *This rejuvenation is quite noticeable after a good psychedelic experience, when, without the dragging weight of physical habit patterns, behavior can be more readily changed.*
>
> *On the other hand, if you make no effort to change, old habits rapidly reassert themselves, and you find yourself sliding back into your previous state. In fact, it can be worse than before, because now you know that things can be better and are disappointed to find yourself mucking around in the same old garbage.*
>
> *Another factor makes this process even more uncomfortable. A lot of energy formerly tied up in repressed material is now released. This energy may be used quite fruitfully to expand the boundaries of your being to new dimensions you have experienced. But if you return to old patterns of behavior, you now have more energy to reinforce them, making life more difficult. For this reason, these experiences must not be taken lightly, but with serious intent....*
>
> *Regardless of the frequency, it is wise to make sure that the previous experience has been well integrated before embarking on the next one. (p. 3-4)*

In short, no matter what brings you to visionary plant medicine work, the ceremonial experience is *only the starting point* for actualizing your healing, awakening, and personal growth. Integration becomes the crucial next step for bringing the teachings of the plants through into the living of your daily life so that you walk the teachings in every moment.

WHAT IS VISIONARY PLANT MEDICINE INTEGRATION?

Visionary plant medicine integration is the process by which a visionary plant medicine practitioner is transformed by the teachings, visions, and experiences from visionary plant medicine experiences and incorporates those changes into daily life. Visionary plant medicine integration can often necessitate attending to traumas to release them fully; understanding the manifestations of ego in one's day-to-day experience; and, practicing new ways of thinking, conceptualizing, and being that are in alignment with wisdom teachings.

WHAT YOU NEED TO KNOW ABOUT THE CHALLENGE OF CHANGE

Releasing old patterns means that something has to die and be reborn. We all have this place inside of us that recoils at the thought of death and dying. The ego hates any end to its continuity and will do anything to persist, even if it means resorting to self-destructive or other-destructive behavior.

The ego serves us deeply by being able to give us a sense of personhood in the world and pull together a teeming mass of impulses, thoughts, emotions, and sensations and give us a moderately coherent sense of "I" with which to face the world. In this sense, the ego is very important and helps us function in the everyday world.

Beyond that rudimentary sense of I, however, is a hodgepodge collection of habits of mind, body, and feelings. If our early life was unsupportive or unhealthy in any way, the ego had to develop a work around to get us through until we reached a time and place where we are strong enough to reconstruct ourselves in a healthier way.

With significant, deep, early, and/or chronic traumas, the workarounds we develop are wired in tightly into the oldest parts of our ego and often go unchallenged for much of our lives, even if they are self-destructive or profoundly unhealthy. These workarounds become deeply embedded patterns that play on repeat over and over again.

Many never reach a place in their lives where they are secure enough to face these deep patterns head on. Not being able to face these patterns head on occurs often because the right kind of support doesn't become available and so life continues as best it can while colliding with the unhealthy pattern over and over again. Not turning towards these patterns is hampered by our social milieu. Our current Western social structures also often reinforce habits of turning away from our deeper patterns through the pressures of modern stress, lack of education regarding emotional and psychological health, and the discounting of the importance of such work as well as through the incredible amount of distraction our information age offers.

The challenge to the ego is simple: These patterns provide a continuity of self. The ego literally is able to recognize itself by experiencing these patterns repeating. Physiologically speaking even, the body rewards the pattern repeating with a nice hit of dopamine, putting even more reinforcement behind the pattern itself. When the ego sees the pattern happening, it says, "Hey that's me. I exist." And, the ego wants to exist. When the ego feels like it doesn't exist, it becomes disturbed. Psychologically speaking this could look like psychosis and/or feel like one is losing their mind and all touch with reality or this could feel like existential discomfort.

So, it does not matter that the egoic house of cards is built on a shoddy foundation. The ego much prefers to continue to stack the cards up than replacing the foundation. Replacing the rotted foundation is equated to death, and death is perceived as highly threatening.

This dynamic in the ego proves to be the most challenging aspect of moving into healthy patterns and letting go of that in our lives that which is generally not serving us. Letting go of those patterns means throwing our ego into what it sees as the arms of death. It also means losing that physiological dopamine-reward-carrot and can even mean feeling withdrawal from the old, self-destructive pattern. What this means is that we have to be strong enough when we want to change for the better.

We have to support our bodies with clean water, nourishing food and supplements, exercise/movement, sunshine, and fresh air. Finding ways to feel pleasure and enjoy life are also critical so we can experience the raw beauty around us. We have to support ourselves emotionally and mentally with a network of caregivers and/or friends and family that can believe in the "new" us before the new us is made manifest. We often do not need large numbers of cheerleaders and helpers, but we need at least a few solid folks that can have our back as we face our "little deaths." We also have to commit to hanging in there with ourselves when our egos are screaming, "NO!" Hanging in there means having ways we can self-support. Various personal practices and disciplines such as meditation, visualization, and breathing/breathwork can be extremely helpful in this regard.

Death feels awful. It's messy. It's painful. But awful, messy, painful, ugliness is no reason to turn back. On the other side of death is Life. It's the place of living from our essential Self, it's the place of living our soul's path. It's the place of being healthy and whole. All of that rotted foundation and house of cards has to go so that we have space to build on solid ground, the right way. You will grieve that which is dying. Feelings of loss, sadness, depression, and confusion naturally arise as part of this process.

The goal of change is never to destroy the ego entirely. In deep personal change, we are freeing the ego from outdated modes of thinking, feeling, and behaving in order for more coherent and integrated patterns to emerge and become rote.

SPIRITUAL BYPASSING: WHAT YOU NEED TO KNOW

Spiritual bypassing is an idea coined by John Welwood that refers to the "use of spiritual practices and beliefs to avoid dealing with our painful feelings, unresolved wounds, and developmental needs" (Masters, 2010, p. 1). As you can imagine, most of us want to find a way not to feel our pain. If we are spiritual seekers, we may find a very clever strategy to avoid and numb our pain through the use of spiritual practices.

While s`piritual bypassing has many forms, the most popular forms for visionary plant medicine users likely include delusions of having arrived at a more advanced level of being, devaluation of the personal relative to the spiritual, and overemphasis on the positive (Masters, 2010).

As Robert Augustus Masters (2010) so aptly writes, "True spirituality is not a high, not a rush, not an altered state.... Authentic spirituality is a vast fire of liberation, an exquisitely fitting crucible and sanctuary, providing both heat and light for the healing we need" (p. 3). We must address all levels of our development if we are to stay grounded and open authentically to the healing and integration that leads to wholeness. Aspects we need to focus on include physical, psychological, emotional, spiritual, relational/social dimensions (Masters, 2010).

The importance of psychological and emotional healing cannot be overstated. For the most part, psychological and emotional issues cannot be worked out with spiritual practice alone. No amount of meditating is going to resolve your strained relationships with your family of origin, for example. Unfortunately, many spiritual practices in this case will only promote spiritual bypassing. Masters (2010) discredits the idea high quality psychotherapy is any less superior to spiritual practice – it is not "lower" or more "inferior" (p. 4).

The key to spiritual bypassing seems to be the desire to avoid pain and suffering and attempting to use spiritual practice to do so. As Masters (2010) explains

> *When transcendence of our personal history takes precedence over intimacy with our personal history, spiritual bypassing is inevitable.... Cutting through spiritual bypassing means turning toward the painful, disfigured, ostracized, unwanted, or otherwise disowned aspects of ourselves and cultivating as much intimacy as possible with them.... If doing so seems to break our heart, we are on the right path, even if we are on our hands and knees. For when our heart breaks, it doesn't shatter; it breaks open, expanding to include more and more.... It would be an understatement to say that this is a challenging journey, for it asks of us a very deep*

vulnerability, a bareness of being to which we may not be at all accustomed. (pp. 12-13)

A mature view of spirituality means "no escape, no need for escape, and utter freedom *through* limitation and every sort of difficulty" (Masters, 2010, p. 42). Steering our ship right into the heart of our pain means engaging in shadow work, defined by Masters (2010) as "the practice of acknowledging, facing, engaging, and integrating what we have turned away from, disowned, or otherwise rejected in ourselves" (p. 43).

One of the motivations for visionary plant medicine use that I hear and read of frequently is the desire to fast track spiritual growth and/or healing. The idea is that one can reach the same state as someone who has meditated for 40 years, for example, in a single evening. Why sit in meditation for decades when a plant teacher can take you there in a matter of minutes or hours? The rationale seems logical on its face, especially when a number of indigenous traditions have used these technologies for hundreds of years, if not longer. Unfortunately, visiting a state of "enlightenment" for a few minutes or hours is

akin to saying that we have reached the top of Mount Everest when in fact we've just been comfortably helicoptered there for a brief, well-insulated landing. Not having taken the climb, and thus not engaged in any of the lessons of such a challenging trek, leaves us far less capable of appreciating where we are than if we had actually made the climb. Our helicoptered

> *self has found a shortcut, but in so doing so has lost out on the grounding and embodiment and participatory knowingness that can be gained only through the climb itself.... Theoretically we may have arrived, but with so little of ourselves actually there, we cannot call it a true arrival.* (Masters, 2010, p. 39)

Trying to take shortcuts only prolongs the process of true psychospiritual healing and development. At a certain point of understanding, you realize that time is basically irrelevant. The process takes as long as it takes, and there is no value judgment placed on the time taken. When we get really real with ourselves and our desire to shortcut, we usually undercover a desire to avoid or limit pain felt. When we can relax into the knowing that taking steps forward and into our shadow is all that is required, the path becomes simple – not easy but simple nonetheless.

In short, spiritual bypassing, or using spiritual practices as ways to avoid facing and healing pain, is uprooted by taking an active stance to engage with shadow elements. As will be discussed in later chapters, working with an expert guide to resolve traumas is my recommendation for managing the natural tendency to spiritually bypass.

DIFFERENCES IN TRADITIONAL MESTIZO AND ABORIGINAL VERSUS MODERN WESTERN USE IN VISIONARY PLANT MEDICINE IN THE AMERICAS

It is important to understand that traditional forms of visionary plant use by mestizo[1] and indigenous populations often had different goals in mind than Western (or Northern American) practitioners do (Winkelman, 2007). Anthropological studies (Saez, 2014) note that ayahuasca, for instance, can create social connections that range from facilitating new patron-client relationships to warfare, either starting a war or as a substitute for one (Labate, Cavnar, & Freedman, 2014; Saez, 2014). Psilocybe mushrooms were used for physical maladies such as fever, chills, acne, and toothache along with cultural-bound syndromes including soul loss, witchcraft, and hexes (Winkelman, 2007).

While a mestizo or indigenous practitioner might be seeking help with "supernatural predation and magical aggressions" (Saez, 2014, p. xxiv); building ethnic alliances and political strategies to confront marginalization (Labate, Cavnar, & Freedman, 2014) and new social relations (Virtanen, 2012); recovery of indigenous cultures (Labate, Cavnar, & Freedman, 2014; Virtanen, 2014); and, hunting (Shepard, 2014) as well as illnesses (Virtanen, 2014), the Western practitioner often seeks self-explora-

---

1 Referring to those of a mixed ancestry of indigenous and typically Western European

tion, spiritual growth, and physical and emotional healing (Brabec de Mori, 2014; Fotiou, 2014; Labate, Cavnar, & Freedman, 2014; Langdon & Santana de Rose, 2014; Saez, 2014). Winkelman (2007) notes that Westerners seek help with spiritual development, emotional healing and unresolved trauma, connecting with the sacred, and personal awareness development. Westerners assume that they will gain "increased self awareness, personal insights, and access to deeper levels of the self that enhanced personal development and expressions of the higher self, providing direction in life" (Winkelman, 2007, pp. 163-64).

As Labate et al., (2014) writes,

> *Grassroots Amazonian shamans have to contend with an uneasy transition from traditional ayahuasca shamanism, including divination, sorcery, and curing sorcery-inflicted wounds, to using ayahuasca for self-exploration and to cater to Westerner's hopes of healing both physical and emotional ailments. Simultaneously, they are involved, either directly or indirectly, in local interethnic exchanges among indigenous groups (p. 8)*

With these two very different goals in mind, we can understand why the process of use by indigenous/mestizo populations could be very different from that of the Westerner (Losonczy & Cappo, 2014). These differing goals and radically different settings and cultural contexts would seem to necessitate different ways of working with these medicines effectively. I argue that the Western practitioner cannot effectively adopt the visionary plant medicine practices of native/mestizo tribes without modification. Our lifestyles, cultural contexts, social conditioning, needs, histories, mentality, and goals for use are simply too divergent.

For me these divergent traditions and histories of use of visionary plants mean that Western (Northern American) practitioners of visionary plant medicine are best to align with culturally akin mediators who can help translate and situate their experiences in ways that help them achieve their goals for healing and self-exploration.

THE SEDUCTION INTO VISIONARY WORLDS

I see many people becoming assimilated into the vegetal world. They go from ceremony to ceremony, as often as twice a month or more. Their lives become completely wrapped up in the worlds of ayahuasca or San Pedro, et cetera, and they move farther and farther away from realizing that they have, perhaps, become lost in a world made to visit but not to inhabit.

Assimilation by the vegetal world is common. The plants have a strong desire for you to be a part of their world. Without realizing it, part of your psyche can begin to think that it is a plant. This confusion can propel you unconsciously to continue your visionary plant medicine activity without questioning frequency of use and/or whether you are integrating the teachings and visions you have received.

I was fortunate that I had three separate healers that I trusted reflect back to me that I had become assimilated into the vegetal world. One healer had to remind my body consciousness that it was not a plant. Another healer reminded my mind that the vegetal world was only one of several levels of consciousness to master. And, the third confirmed for me that the plants do possess these assimilation qualities.

Another strong aspect of seduction into visionary plant medicine circles is the strong desire humans have for connection, love, and belonging. These topics have been written about widely. Abraham Maslow (Daniels, 2013) strongly identified these needs as part of his famous hierarchy of needs popularized through the humanistic school of psychology. More recently, social work researcher, author, and speaker Brené Brown (2012, 2015) deeply explores these needs as part of the essential fabric of humanity and our sense of wholeness. Modern attachment theorists such as David Wallin (2007) and Dan Siegel (2001, 2003, 2007) note their importance for psychological health and wellbeing.

The tribal nature of most ceremonies uses a set and setting that we are deeply familiar with on a base human level and one that is profoundly appealing to a Western psyche (Fotiou, 2014; Walsh & Grob, 2007). As one of my teachers Malidoma Patrice Some said, we know it in our bones. Being outdoors, sitting in a circle, being in a group, joined in the middle with a fire, flanked by an altar, and serenaded by music calls us back to a time when we all lived in tribes, close to the earth and the elements, and in communion with our surroundings.

A challenge for the modern psyche is that while the tribal perspective is deeply appealing, "we must not idealize it" (Goldsmith, 2007, p. 125). The tribal perspective is not more evolved than our modern one. The promised land is actually the postmodern, or post postmodern, perspective that "accommodates the material and the spiritual, already split by modernity, by reuniting them via a transcendence of their duality—an integral perspective" (Goldsmith, 2007, p. 125).

My experience of visionary plant medicine practice was a deep awakening to a feeling of connection, love, and belonging that was aided by the tribal set and setting but that also went beyond it. Longing for this ancient familiarity can be deep, especially when we lack a deep feeling of love, belonging, and connection in our own day-to-day lives. If we lack these feelings, we can find ourselves returning to visionary plant medicine not because we need it for our growth and/or healing, but because it is temporarily filling a void we have and/or helping us "take the edge off" of the pain we feel regularly. To know whether your visionary plant medicine practice is temporarily filling a void or helping you heal requires a deep level of discernment and, often, outside expert guidance.

STATES AND STAGES OF CONSCIOUSNESS AND THE HEALING POWER OF ALTERED STATES OF CONSCIOUSNESS

One of the age-old discussions in the psychedelic world and the transpersonal world more generally is the differentiation between states of consciousness and stages of consciousness. For the uninitiated, there can be quite a bit of confusion between the two. A state of consciousness is temporary. A stage of consciousness is more permanent. Both states and stages can change and evolve. We go through many states of consciousness throughout our day from sleeping, waking, dreaming, meditating, and the like. Stages of consciousness would refer more to developmental structures that are more long lasting. We can experience states of consciousness in whatever stage of consciousness we are in.

It is widely known that children go through clear developmental stages. In the West, in the latter half of the 20th Century, scientists and philosophers began examining stages of adult development after realizing that adults do in fact develop (Coder, 2011). A number of psychologists and researchers have created models of adult development which detail the various developmental stages adults can experience in their maturation process (Cook-Greuter, 2005; Wilber, 2001, 2006, 2007). Higher, or more inclusive, levels of egoic development enable individuals to perform increasingly difficult operations in their daily lives based on the ability to operate from greater degrees of abstraction (Cook-Greuter, 2005). Higher levels of development also indicate movement towards advanced stages of consciousness, sometimes referred to as enlightenment (Coder, 2011).

There has been an ongoing debate about whether a state-based experience can advance a person to a higher stage of development. Experiencing a state of consciousness does not mean that one resides in a corresponding stage of consciousness. For example, you can have a unitive experience during a visionary plant medicine ceremony but that does not mean that you have attained a unitive stage of egoic development.

Part of the challenge of experiencing states of consciousness far outside of one's "home base" stage of consciousness/egoic development is that it can lead a person to believe that they have achieved that more encompassing (read more advanced) stage of consciousness well before that stage of development has been reached (Goldsmith, 2007). This form of delusion can lead to many challenges as you might imagine including levels of self-aggrandizement, confusion as to what personal work is needed, narcissism, denial of shadow elements at play in oneself and so forth.

The ego is a very tricky animal and it will want to grab onto any sense of elevation or advancement as proof that nothing in the egoic realm needs to change. The ego can even use these state-based experiences to defend itself against further inward inquiry and shadow work and can ultimately stymie your healing and integration process.

As they say, what goes up must come down. Know that coming down from any state reached through visionary plant medicine is a necessary part of the process. You have not "lost" anything. You are simply arriving back where you were before, hopefully taking with you some valuable treasures and reference points that can help spur your integration process forward.

Having said that, there is support for the healing power of altered states of consciousness (ASC) from visionary plant medicine (House, 2007; Winkelman, 2007). As Winkelman (2007) writes

> *These ASC experiences allow for the emergence of primary process thinking in visual symbols which allow for manifestation of emotional and social dynamics from pre-egoic levels where developmental blockages occurred. This emergence provides content for the management of social and personal attachments and emotions and the transfer from the unconscious into consciousness, enhancing awareness of one's own psychodynamics.*
>
> *Visionary experiences are diagnostic, providing content and structure reflective of the client's current needs for psychological growth. Visions manifest repressed energies, unresolved conflicts, and developmental dynamics, often manifested in archetypal images that... link back into earlier trauma and forward to the next developmental stage.... The psychotherapeutic processes that incorporate these*

foundational shamanic images (archetypes) heal by connecting psyche with its ancient natural roots and energy for healing, providing a sense of wholeness and connectedness.... The symbolic emergence of the unconscious material allows for individuation (producing a psychologically whole and integrated consciousness) to occur outside of conscious awareness. Journeying accelerates development by symbolic elevation of this embedded material into personal consciousness where it can transform self-awareness. (pp. 161-62).

House (2007) notes that the ASC from psychedelics seems to facilitate insight "through their ability to suspend one's usual defense mechanisms, allowing greater self-awareness, or openness" (p. 177). Walsh and Grob (2007) noted that this ASC engenders "a deep experiencing and acceptance of whatever experiences arose" (p. 218) that is capable of metabolizing and transforming.

A NOTE ON INDIVIDUATION, MATURATION, AND THE ATTAINMENT OF PERSONAL SOVEREIGNTY AND RELATIONALITY

This introduction would not be complete without a special note to personal sovereignty and relationality.

I am including these concepts in this guidebook as I find them to be one of the largest gifts of the work of integration. As we become more whole – or at least experience ourselves consistently as whole, we begin to move into more advanced degrees of personal autonomy, capable of ruling our inner landscape with much more freedom than was ever possible beforehand. We also are able to relax into relatedness to a degree not formerly felt. As our backlog of traumas and points of incompleteness find resolution and finally heal, the profound process of individuation and maturation becomes more firmly rooted, and we can express our more essential nature more openly and easily (Frager & Fadiman, 1984).

Visionary plant medicine often shows us what the place of individuation and maturation feels like (or looks like), and the hope is that we will engage in the deeper work of integration so that these phenomena become our lived realities rather than momentary experiences.

The place of individuation and personal maturity is what you have been seeking. It's what your Soul is calling you into. It's what led you to the plants and healing work to begin with. This is the goal.

DEFINE YOUR INTENTION FOR VISIONARY PLANT MEDICINE PRACTICE

Having stated my view, however, I would add that each visionary plant medicine practitioner is best served to understand their intention of visionary plant medicine practice (Goldsmith, 2007; House, 2007). What goals are you trying to reach in this practice? What are you trying to heal and/or understand? Are you intending to awaken spiritually?

Personally, I began working with visionary plant medicine in order to heal deep-seated trauma that I had not been able to reach any other way. I received some unexpected side benefits that included the unlocking of various healing gifts, a deeper embodied understanding of ultimate reality, and realizations into delusions perpetuated by the ego, among others.

All of these teachings have been helpful to me, and many mirrored teachings I had received through various spiritual teachers and other mystical experiences I had previously. However, my deepest desire in working with visionary plant medicine was not to receive the teachings over and over again. My deepest desire has been liberation from the dominance of my traumatized egoic consciousness and, thus, to be able to live the paradoxically simultaneous, sacred and profane.

The point for me with visionary plant medicine work was always how to integrate those teachings into daily, mundane life. I find that the most power resides in living those teachings day in and day out, not simply experiencing them in altered states of consciousness. In the words of Alan Watts (2013), "Such aids to perception are medicines, not diets, and... the use of a medicine should lead on to a more healthful mode of living" (p. 82).

ARE YOU OVERDOING IT?

If you cannot live without altering your reality drastically on a frequent basis, you may have missed the point of the teachings of visionary plant medicine. Ask yourself the following questions:

- Are you sitting in ceremony for more than once a month or once every several months?
- If you have attended a longer, multi-ceremony retreat, did you take several months or longer to integrate the work?
- When you feel disturbed in your life, is your first thought that you need another ceremony?
- Do you reach out to expert healers beyond the ceremonial container to help you integrate?
- Do you have practices in place to help you integrate?

As part of this inquiry, reflect on whether you have been seduced by the visions or assimilated by the plants as part of your effort to heal and awaken. If you suspect that you have been "seduced" or assimilated, it's time to take a serious break from visionary plant medicine and integrate deeply. I advise in this way not to shame you but to help awaken you to finding balance with this work so that you do not get stuck somewhere that may feel good but that which ultimately does not serve your deeper journey to arrive at awakened sovereignty and wholeness.

As House (2007) writes, "The point is not to have psychedelic visions over and over but to learn how to put them into practice" (p. 183). As one of House's (2007) study participants noted, "The medicine work is like finding the next level of messages. Then [I had] to come back to ordinary reality and ground it. [And,] find ways to work in everyday life" (p. 184).

THE 10 KEYS TO INTEGRATE VISIONARY PLANT MEDICINE EXPERIENCES

Undergoing a major alteration of consciousness with visionary plants is a big decision that requires careful consideration. Returning to your world anew with the teachings from plant medicine deserves even more care and attention so that you can fully receive the gifts offered.

In your time of integration, the following activities are highly advantageous to your growth and healing:

- Expert Guidance
- Trauma Release
- Spiritual Discipline and Practices
- Reflection, Inner Listening and Creativity
- Meaning Making
- Spaciousness and Time
- Nature and Grounding
- Adequate Physical Care (Diet, Exercise/Movement, and Rest)

- Cultivating Virtues
- Turning Outward: Returning to the World

In the following guidebook, I will cover each of these points separately so that you have a trustworthy road map for your journey Home. I wish you very well on this remarkable, albeit windy road of personal healing, integration, and individuation.

CHAPTER 2

....

EXPERT GUIDANCE

Men anpil, chay pa lou.
Many hands make the load lighter.

—Haitian Proverb

Anyone who has worked with visionary plant medicine knows that many revelations, teachings and healings can come through the visions and experiences that one has in ceremony. Many times, these visions can be confusing, and you may not be sure how to interpret what you saw and felt.

What is true is that we interpret the visions from our current state of consciousness outside of the ceremony. Generally speaking, the more developed you are spiritually and egoistically, the less distorted your interpretations may be. This is true because you have greater clarity.

Most of the time the ego subverts the interpretation process to suit its inherent needs for continuity. Therefore, your interpretation of what happened is filtered through your historical lens and through any points of traumatic experience you may have had. As the ego sees through the past and through its lens of fear, often our interpretations are quite distorted. This is all to say that you cannot always trust your interpretation (Hollis, 2005).

Other times, you may have experienced a profound teaching or vision that you are not sure how to integrate into your life. Being shown that you are depressed is one thing, but recovering from depression is another! In all of these cases, you may need to reach out to an expert (or experts) for further support to help you understand what happened and how to heal fully.

In many cases, experts in energy clearing, psychological healing, physiological healing, and bodywork may be required to help you integrate. These experts can be energy healers, acupuncturists, psychologists/psychotherapists, somatic therapists, and those in similar professions.

While the ceremony may happen on a single night (or over the course of a week-long retreat), you likely will need consistent care by an expert guide following your visionary plant medicine immersion. Weeks, months, and sometimes years of support may be required depending on the depth of healing and integration needed.

Consistent care with an expert offers you the ability to unwind the "knots" and conditioning in your system that landed you in the arms of visionary plant medicine to begin with. Our physical bodies need time and sustained practice of the new way to rewire so that you can move into a new stage of consciousness.

It can be helpful to choose a guide/healer/expert practitioner who has experiences with visionary plant medicine, but it is not necessary. If you choose to work with a psychologist or psychotherapist, I would recommend that you choose someone experienced with visionary plant medicine and hallucinogens or someone who is not biased against them as their own fear and bias may get projected onto you as part of the therapeutic process.[2] As for bodyworkers, acupuncturists, energy healers, and the like, visionary plant medicine experience is less necessary as they are attending to more physical and energetic aspects of your being. However, with the rise of visionary plant medicine use, many of such healers may have encountered the energetic signatures of visionary plant medicine and may be able to work with their effects specifically as well.

The following is a partial list of the types of revelations through visionary plant medicine of which you would want to seek expert guidance:

- Abuse (physical, emotional, psychological, verbal, and sexual)
- Addiction
- Preverbal wounding/trauma
- Trauma/PTSD

---

[2] MAPS provides a list of visionary plant medicine -friendly expert practitioners here.

- Depression/dysthymia
- Anxiety
- Relational wounding/challenges
- Disordered thinking patterns (unhealthy/rigid belief structures)
- Emotional dysregulation including emotional disconnection
- Isolation
- Sleep disturbance
- Paranoid and/or delusional thoughts
- Psychic attack/Energetic parasites
- Mania/hypomania
- Suicidality or Self Harming thoughts
- *Susto*[3]

Of those conditions mentioned, suicidality, mania/hypomania, abuse, PTSD, depression, delusional and paranoid thoughts, disrupted sleep, addiction, *susto*, and psychic attack are the most severe, and professional help should be sought out immediately.

In addition, any condition after a visionary plant medicine ceremony where you feel like you have not made it

---

3 *Susto* is a culturally bound condition that is most common in Latin American women after an experience of trauma or proximity to someone else who was traumatized. The translation in English is "fright." *Susto* has also been described in more shamanic terms as "soul loss," or a "tear in the soul." In this condition, a person will have trouble recognizing themselves. They experience a loss of meaning, passion, and engagement. Anhedonia can be present as well as feelings of sadness, hopelessness, despair, and depression. See Winkelman (2007, p. 151) and Bombaci (2014).

back yet (or have not fully returned) should be attended to immediately as well. It can be dangerous to have part of your consciousness outside of your body as you will lack awareness of what is happening to you and around you at the moment. Sometimes after an intense experience, it can take a few days to fully return. In these cases, please make sure there is a trusted person monitoring you throughout the day. Driving or any like task should be avoided completely.

Keep in mind that if you were part of a tribe that used visionary plant medicine regularly such as those in the Amazon or through the Native American Church, you would be held closely in the tight container of your community where expert guides would be available to you as part of the structure of your society.

In the MDMA-Assisted Psychotherapy Treatment Manual, Mithoefer (2013) notes that therapists are present to answer any questions the participant may have, and to offer support and encouragement as the participant processes the emotional responses and new perceptions resulting from the MDMA assisted session. The therapists take a supportive and validating stance toward the participant's experience. They also help the participant further explore and develop new insights about their trauma, new perspectives about life and relationships, shifts in their relationship to their own emotions and the clearing of old thought patterns and reactions that may have outlived their usefulness. They discuss the meaning of the memories, thoughts, feelings, and insights experienced during the MDMA-assisted sessions and how this new meaning will be manifested in daily living. The therapists may offer insights or interpretations regarding the participant's experience, but this should be minimized. Participants should be encouraged to exercise their own judgment about whether any given comment by the therapists may or may not resonate for them, and to apply their own discernment about what may be applicable and useful to understanding to their experience.

Goldsmith (2007) writes

> We have learned to involve trusted significant others—family, therapist, and physician—in the process of psychedelic psychotherapy. In most contemporary models, significant others communicate with the subject before, are nearby during, and available after a psychedelic treatment. The focus is on the benefit to the participant, and guidance is responsive to request, rather than proactive or directive.... There is some debate as to the wisdom of having a psychedelic experience alone. Clearly, psychotherapy would not be taking place during a solo psychedelic experience. However, profound meditation and introspection generally results and the content of the session could produce significant fodder for subsequent therapeutic discussion and analysis. Even if the choice is made by an experienced adult to have a solitary experience, supportive others should be readily available. (pp. 122-23)

Goldsmith (2007) notes that "many epiphanies are lost and resolutions broken by the 'after-the-marathon-weekend' effect—that is, reentry into the same context in which the problem was developed" (p. 123).

The introduction of visionary plant medicine to Westerners (and Northern Americans) who do not have built-in social structures for visionary plant medicine ceremony and healing experiences is relatively new (less than 50 years old) and necessitates that such persons must create such a structure of containment for themselves. This requires more effort on the part of the Western/Northern American practitioner to identify and commit to receiving adequate guidance to integrate. However, if you are serious about your healing and growth, having adequate containment, guidance, and support is integral to you making the gains you seek. Without that support, you run the risk of psychological and physical endangerment (House, 2007).

House (2007) writes that in the period before full integration occurs, "individuals are at a heightened risk for a variety of psychiatric problems ranging from depression and anxiety to hallucinogen-persisting perceptual disorder" (p. 182). He advises working with a therapist during integration to increase the likelihood of successful integration, noting that a therapist can provide an alternative perspective for insight development.

CHAPTER 3:

....

TRAUMA RELEASE

Love finds it soul in its feelings of incompleteness, impossibility, and imperfection.

—Thomas Moore

Spiritual progress is like detoxification. Things have to come up in order to be released. Once we have asked to be healed, then our unhealed places are forced to the surface.

—Marianne Williamson

Often practitioners of visionary plant medicine will have layers of trauma revealed to them during the course of their work with visionary plant medicine. Childhood wounding, pre-verbal trauma, abuse, and other painful experiences often get revealed to help practitioners begin to understand and release that which is causing them internal turmoil. Sometimes visionary plant medicine practitioners are aware of the trauma and, other times, it is "new" information for them to process.

Often in ceremony, visionary plant medicine practitioners experience purging, or "getting well," shaking, crying, coughing, body movements, yawning, and laughing, among other forms of somatic release, as an aspect of this trauma release.

Why does this occur?

If you imagine all of the experiences you have had personally over the course of your lifetime that you were unable to process fully and make sense of, you can begin to see that there might be quite a lot "backed up" in your energetic body and system that would like to be cleared and resolved.

Now, if you believe that ancestral levels of trauma, or, more generally, points that lack resolution in your familial lineages can also affect your day-to-day experience of life, then there is quite a bit more that desires resolution for a total sense of clarity of being to be present. For example, if your lineage includes enslavement, as many African Americans do, but you personally were never enslaved, then visionary plant medicine work could bring up this lineage-based, or ancestral trauma, for healing. There is more and more support for the idea of ancestral clearing, including empirically based research studies (Bombay, Matheson, & Anisman, 2009; Coyle, 2014; Portney, 2003) so it seems that even modern science supports this aspect of the clearing and integrating process.

Now, if you are open to the idea of past lives, or concurrent lives even, the amount that could want to be processed, reconciled, cleared, and integrated grows exponentially. As you begin to work consciously with clearing and healing in this lifetime, you are likely to encounter a gigantic backlog of trauma that is seeking to be cleared. It can be quite overwhelming to intuit the magnitude of the work to be done!

Those working with many modalities of healing will begin to encounter this backlog. Practitioners of visionary plant medicine are no different.

The confusion that arises for visionary plant medicine practitioners is the degree of trauma resolution provided by "the medicine." Most often, visionary plant medicine begins a process of trauma release that is addressing this backlog of traumatic experience that desires full resolution. However, in most cases, visionary plant medicine does not fully heal our traumas (House, 2007; Naranjo, 1973; Stolaroff, 1993; Strassman, 1997).

As one of House's (2007) study participants commented,

> *I don't believe you can just take the medicines and then that automatically changes you. It might change you some. I think, to really get the benefit of it, it's just a tool that goes along with other tools you can use. (p. 181)*

Most of what I have experienced personally and seen in my client work is that visionary plant medicine opens the door to healing our traumas, but we have to walk through that door to move towards total resolution. Total resolution comes through completing the processes of integration, which often entails the assistance of trained trauma specialists and other expert helpers and through extended periods of reflection, grounding, and meaning-making. All of these processes take time (House, 2007).

There are a few important points to consider in understanding why this is the case.

First, any healing that took place during the ceremony also took place in a state of consciousness very different from your normal waking state of consciousness. It is necessary to bring those "threads of healing" through into your normal waking state of consciousness so that this material is fully processed and integrated.

When in ceremony, we are receiving information from Spirit, unconscious or subconscious parts of ourselves, the shadow, deities, etheric beings, and such. In this space, we can experience revelation and receive information and understanding that was formerly hidden to us. Receiving information from higher realms can feel blissful, intense, magical, and enlivening. We can also receive teachings and information that feels unpleasant and even frightening.

We then take that information and move into the realm of our personhood. We make meaning of the information we have received so that it becomes insight into our condition and helps us understand how we can reconcile ourselves with our wounding. As we move through the process of meaning-making, we bring what we have learned through our physical, emotional, and mental bodies. This means that our physicality has a chance to process this information at the cellular level; our minds have a chance to process the information and integrate it into our mental understanding; and, we have the chance to process the information emotionally, which may result in cathartic feelings of all kinds. This is a key aspect of the integration process. This means that what we receive from visionary plant medicine can be brought all the way through our "many bodies" – physical, emotional, and mental – into a deeper form of embodiment.

In addition to making meaning, we may find that our bodies need to clear old wounds and traumas. Often in ceremony we can receive an awareness of something that we were unaware of previously. Seeing the traumas and pain of our childhood with greater clarity, understanding another key person in our lives more accurately, and receiving instruction on how to live one's life more wholly would all be common examples of what can be revealed with visionary plant medicine. With the traumatic pieces especially, they will be part of a larger constellation of experience that make up some of our behaviors, thoughts, and emotional patterns in our daily lives.

In Jungian terms, this constellation would be called a complex. According to Hollis (2005), a complex is "a cluster of energy in the unconscious, charged by historic events, reinforced through repetition, embodying a fragment of our personality, and generating a programmed response and an implicit set of expectations" (p. 91). Hollis notes that some of our complexes are good in that they enable us to love, trust, and commit in relationships. We move into a complex when an "unconscious stimulus is received" (p. 93), it interacts with a part of our personal history, and that feeling from the historical event(s) is brought to the surface. As this happens, other dynamics such as abandonment, overwhelmment, trust/distrust, and approach/avoid are also brought to the fore.

As Hollis (2005) emphasizes,

> *we do not consciously intend for such repetitions,... but they have a life of their own, and bind us to the narrowness of our history rather than our capacious future, the more so because we are unconscious of their presence and their power. (p. 93)*

In healing that complex, we often have to see how it has affected us. We have to understand its origination point and how it has been re-experienced over and over again as it has been triggered in our lives. We have to see how it has created emotional patterns that we have enacted time and time again. We have to see how it has altered and directed our thought processes. We have to see how it has changed the way we see, feel, and sense our most fundamental sense of selfhood in the world. We have to see how the complex has directed our life – how it has encouraged us to move in the world, in our relationships, our work, and so on (Hollis, 2005). Alternatively, sometimes in visionary plant medicine work as well as other healing modalities, we simply release complexes without fully needing to understand their ramifications and points of origination.

The complex itself will have many threads and, often, we must see these threads fully so that we understand how the trauma has affected us. Once we understand this, we can begin to move towards resolution. We must attend to the mental, emotional, and physical bodies before we can fully resolve our trauma. When we have attended to all of these levels of healing the trauma, the "wound" no longer festers and can finally heal. There may be a scar that shows where the wound was, but we are no longer held captive by the trauma.

It is important to note that our bodies are likely to need a specific type of trauma release that bypasses the rational mind and the meaning-making function. A purely physical release of trauma is explained by the field of Trauma Dynamics (Razvi, 2016) among others (Levine, 1997). The idea is that the body itself needs to complete a release of the original stressor through a more instinctual process. This release can look like shaking, crying, shallow breathing, body movements, and the like. When the body completes its release of the trauma, full resolution becomes possible.

As you can imagine, moving through the depths of these points can take some time, and we may need some expert help along the way! This process of turning deeply towards our pain is also not for the faint of heart (Hollis, 2005).

In the words of Robert Augustus Masters (2010),

> *Turning towards our pain is an act of radical caring—and not just caring for ourselves—because in doing so we cease to fuel our avoidance and those addictive behaviors we have used to keep ourselves from pain.... Turning toward our pain is about bringing into our heart all that we have rejected, ostracized, disowned, neglected, bypassed, shunned, excommunicated, or otherwise deemed unworthy in ourselves. Our heart has room for it all. (p. 53).*

Healing our trauma means facing our shadows – the parts of ourselves and our history that we want to distance ourselves from because of how painful it feels. As we keep turning towards our pain, instead of distancing ourselves from shadowy elements, we can courageously embrace what we have rejected with compassion (Masters, 2010).

> *As we deeply encounter our shadow without losing ourselves in it, we free its energies and develop a genuine intimacy with it, until our shadow is no longer an "it" but rather a reclaimed us. This is true integration, organic and real, felt right to the core, manifesting as a deeply felt sense of wholeness, balance, and integrity. (Masters, 2010, p. 48)*

Second, agency is key. As the Quakers say, "When you pray, move your feet." Full resolution means that we take appropriate responsibility for our healing and we move forward in action to resolve our traumas. No one can do our healing work for us. In the end, we heal ourselves although we can receive help along the way. When the visionary plant medicine shows us what needs to be healed, we are then required to take action to complete the healing process.

I see the healing and trauma resolution process in a similar light. We are the ones we have been waiting for. No one is going to do our trauma work for us. We have to step forward and take the risks despite the uncertainty, despite the places that feel dark and scary, to heal ourselves. Spirit will meet us on this path of action and self-responsibility and will help us, but we have to be our own agent of healing.

This assumption of personal responsibility is a key part of the maturation process. And, as many of you may have witnessed, the plants are asking you to take responsibility – to grow up – so that you can be more capable forces of light, beauty, and truth in a world that desperately needs that. By healing, we live more deeply into the Wholeness that we are and we find a capacity that we did not know existed.

CHAPTER 4:

....

PSYCHOSPIRITUAL DISCIPLINE AND PRACTICES

Before enlightenment, chop wood, carry water. After enlightenment, chop wood, carry water.

—Zen Proverb

A spiritual experience induced out of context of the rest of one's life and history is like a cut flower: beautiful, but with no prepared foundation in which to root and grow, doomed to fade.

—Neal Goldsmith

Regular contemplative practice is recommended in the practice of many religious and spiritual traditions. Contemplative practice can include prayer, meditation, singing, yoga, mantra work, and other similar practices that encourage connection to something greater, dissolution of egoic attachment, and inner strengthening.

I recommend consistent contemplative practice for visionary plant medicine communities as it supports connection with one's inner life, reflection, contact with deeper truths, neurological balancing and growth, and virtues such as patience, discipline, perseverance, humility, and compassion.

The Zen parable speaks of practice before and after enlightenment as being the same. Chop wood and carry water before and after realization. To me this parable speaks of the grounding nature of daily contemplative practice and the needs of our human minds, bodies, and psyches for contact with inner reality, both personal and transpersonal.

Often the altered states of consciousness induced by visionary plant medicine are extreme. As such, there is a wide gap between what we experience in those altered states and what we experience in our daily lives. Consistent contemplative practice helps form the bridge between these worlds – between these altered states of consciousness so that our psyches and bodies can begin to make sense of what we experienced and integrate it fully.

In addition to the reinforcement of this bridge between visionary states and normal waking consciousness, spiritual disciplines provide ethical guidelines and a values base from which to operate.

As Myron Stolaroff (1993) writes

> *Experts in the field now generally agree that it is wise to conduct psychedelic explorations within the framework of a spiritual discipline or growth program that will continually call attention to fundamental values and goals. A good discipline will outline a body of ethics for personal behavior that will support the changes required. Good ethics will also help us stay clear about our objectives, and will keep the door open to increasing depths of experience. (p. 3)*

Goldsmith (2007) supports Stolaroff's assertion, stating that "psychedelics generally do not effect 'cures,' gains in psychological peace and spiritual maturity must be maintained with the support of an ongoing practice" (p. 124).

Often what you will experience in the visionary states guides you to areas of your life that need work. As the Entheogenic Research Integration (ERIE) Foundation (ERIE, n.d.) suggests, it is very helpful to create a practice from your experience that you can then use in your daily life to initiate and reinforce the change you are making.

Once again, the challenge that most novice and sometimes even more experienced visionary plant medicine practitioners have is thinking that the plant has already healed them, and, therefore, the work is already done. For example, a practitioner working with psilocybin mushrooms has the intention of deeply healing her childhood. The mushrooms then show a time when her younger child self was crying in a corner alone. The words come,

"No one loves me," and she sees herself leaving that child in the corner unsure how to help her.

The key information here would be realizing that there is a part of the inner child that is wounded and feels abandoned. Most likely that part of the inner child is still acting out in this practitioner's day-to-day life as threats of abandonment arise. In addition to seeking help to speak more thoroughly about what happened in childhood that produced this situation, this practitioner could add a practice to her life to notice when she is feeling abandoned and then speak to the inner child to let her know that she is being cared for. This kind of practice would help this part of the inner child integrate back into the practitioner's total sense of self.

Of course there are other practices that could be developed in this example, and the most important point about a practice is that it makes sense and is meaningful to the one practicing it. You also want a practice that you can commit to doing regularly – everyday perhaps! Working with an expert or highly knowledgeable peers can help you find the right practices if you are unsure which direction to turn. An expert can also help you stay accountable to your practices and also help you learn from the practice itself so that your growth work is receiving adequate guidance and support.

In considering deep psychospiritual practices, literature and research from transpersonal psychology point to a category of encompassing practices called *psychospiritual integrative practices* (Wall, Nye, & FitzMedrud, 2013) that aim to transform the practitioner. In shorthand, integrative means attending to body, heart, mind, and spirit according to Cortright, Kahn, and Hess (2003). Transformation is seen to mean profound changes in consciousness of the practitioner (Luskin, 2004) or shifts in worldview with accompanying changes in core values (Schiltz, Vieten, & Amorok, 2007). Wall, Nye, and FitzMedrud (2013) state that Passage Meditation, the Hoffman Quadrinity Process, Integral Transformative Practice, Mindfulness Based Stress Reduction, prayer, yoga, Transcendental Meditation, and qigong are all forms of psychospiritual integrative practices. I would recommend working with one of these practices if you are adding a spiritual practice/discipline to your routine.

A SPECIAL NOTE ON MEDITATION AS A PRACTICE

There have been numerous studies on the effects of meditation on physiology, psychology, and social experience (MacDonald, Walsh, & Shapiro, 2013). A summary of the findings of this research indicates that physiologically, meditation changes the way the brain and body function. Meditation seems to improve stress responses and generate "greater state and trait expressions of calmness and relaxedness as seen in a variety of body systems" (MacDonald et al., 2013, p. 439) including respiratory, endocrine, and blood/circulatory systems. Neurologicallyoriented research also shows improved "integration and harmonization of brain structure activation" (MacDonald et al., 2013, p. 439-40), greater control over executive functions, better affect regulation, and increased automatic processing. Studies also show that brain structures may also change in size, density, and efficiency.

Psychosocial studies on meditation show a wide variety of improvements in psychological and social functioning engendered by these practices (MacDonald et al., 2013). Examples of these changes include improved learning capacities, concentration, perceived self-control, self-esteem, empathy, creativity, maturation, coping skills, and emotional intelligence. Interestingly enough, research suggests that meditation-oriented practices have improved effects if they are practiced within a spiritual container rather than in a secular format (MacDonald et al., 2013).

It is important to note that meditation practices have also been seen to be unhealthy for those with psychiatric illness and for others who have no diagnosable condition (Rocha, 2014). Meditation, and contemplative practice more broadly, has been seen to initiate what is called the dark night of the soul, which has resulted in suicides, psychotic breaks, mental illness, and profound periods of personal dysregulation. A Buddhist teacher, Shinzen Young, notes that it can take months or years to "fully metabolize" a dark night experience (Rocha, 2014, n.p.).

CHAPTER 5

....

REFLECTION, INNER LISTENING, AND CREATIVE EXPRESSION

Your vision will become clear only when you can look into your own heart. Who looks outside, dreams; who looks inside, awakes.

—Carl Jung

The previous sections on expert guidance, trauma resolution, and spiritual discipline and practices all point to the need for inner reflection and listening. I cannot stress these two points of integration highly enough.

From the time we were very little, we have been looking outside of ourselves for guidance and knowledge. We encountered a world that felt much larger and more powerful than we seemed to be (Hollis, 2005). We needed others outside of ourselves to survive. By design it seems, we had to rely on others to reflect back critical aspects of our inner hardware so that we could see them and actualize them within ourselves (Firman & Gila, 1997).

All of these factors set us up to be looking outside ourselves for almost everything. We learned to listen to our teachers in school, bosses and colleagues at work, our family for various life happenings, the media for what is happening in the world, politicians and pundits for what is happening in our country and internationally, religious and spiritual leaders for how to live our lives, doctors for how to be healthy, and our friends and partners for all of the above and more.

We have been trained intensely on how to listen to the outside world.

The training that is of fundamental importance in the path of integration and maturation is how to listen inwardly. What do we feel, think, sense, know, understand, intuit and so on?

Forms of meditation can be wonderful tools for inner listening as we become aware of what is arising from moment to moment. Other tools that are helpful include journaling, art making, dreamwork, and forms of therapy that promote inner awareness (Mithoefer, 2013). Counseling, for instance, if it is done with a therapist that can help you probe into your inner world can be enormously useful and generative. Forms of bodywork can be useful too if they promote a deeper listening to the body itself.

The body is a wonderful resource for understanding one's inner landscape more deeply.

We must learn to listen to our inner world to move towards greater personal maturity and healing because we are the only ones who really know what we need. No one is walking our path but us, and others' paths are their own. Your path is unique and individual to you.

Our own inner guidance is what tells us what is true for us and what is right for us. We can often be scared to listen to our inner guidance as it has not yet become a source we trust. This is normal at first because it takes practice to get to know the voice of our inner guidance and to trust it to lead us to the right path for us.

When we are able to listen to this source of guidance and assistance, we are able to stay more fully on our path, taking fewer deviations to check out others' worlds and paths. We are able to begin trusting ourselves more and assessing more soberly the advice of others along the way. We are able to feel into whether our bodies support certain moves, teachings, ideas, and people or oppose them. We can know whether we feel a deeper alignment with choices that arise in our path or not.

In terms of our work with visionary plant medicine, a developed sense of inner listening is critical when receiving the teachings of the plants. When we already know how to listen to ourselves, we can much more easily hear the plants. And, once we have landed back on earth after the ceremony, we can listen to ourselves in order to make meaning of the experience rather than adopt someone else's opinion on what happened to us.

A practice of inner listening and reflecting post-ceremony and pre-ceremony is necessary. Like a set of Russian nesting dolls, there are many layers to any experience with visionary plant medicine. Our first takeaways are often just the beginning of understanding what has transpired and what it means. The meaning continues to evolve as the process of reflection deepens. Five years after a powerful experience with visionary plant medicine, you may have a completely different understanding of what it meant. By continuing to listen inwardly and reflect, you tend to the garden of that living meaning-making process.

Being able to listen inwardly also shows us what the next steps are in the healing and integration journey. For example, if we discover in a visionary plant medicine ceremony that we have abused marijuana unknowingly, we can begin to take the steps forward to heal. As part of that healing, we may hear our bodies telling us that our organs feel tired and need a cleanse to help them purify the remains of the marijuana residue. As we heal further, we may notice that without using marijuana, we feel a base level of anxiety and insecurity in the world that surfaces as a jittery feeling frequently in our everyday experience of life. As we attend to the underlying insecurity, we may listen in and realize that we chose to use marijuana because we were deeply troubled as a young teenager by the abusive home we grew up in and choose marijuana to take the edge off that discomfort. We then can begin to work through the pain of the challenges that we felt in our early home life.

As you can see from this example, the process of listening provides us with the next breadcrumbs of work that needs to be done in order to fully heal.

As such, making a place for the practice of inner listening and reflection is a crucial part of the integration journey. You must find ways to self-reflect with discernment and hear what your essential self is saying to you. You must hear what your body wants to share. And, we often must hear what we have been closing our ears off to all of the time before as well as when our own internal chatter is leading us astray. As you grow stronger in your listening, you will gain strength to hear the unpleasant as you will have practiced that many times over!

CHAPTER 6

....

MEANING MAKING

Our greatest freedom is the freedom to choose our attitude.

—Viktor Frankl

Wisdom is found only in truth.

—Johann Wolfgang von Goethe

As was referenced many times previously, the process of meaning making is a fundamental aspect of the visionary plant medicine journey and the process of integration and healing. What is meaning making? Meaning making can be put simply as the story we tell ourselves about what happened.

There are innumerable stories we could create in any moment. Most of our stories are based on personal history. Our history is made up of what happened to us, and, perhaps more importantly, how we interpreted what happened to us. Our memories are layered concoctions, a weaving of objective reality, personal interpretation, and emotion.

The challenge in our personal histories is that our childhood brains were often not great interpreters of meaning. What I mean by that is that children tend to internalize and over-ascribe personal responsibility for events that occurred. This stems from the standard phases of development that children go through that coincide with deficits in the ability to reason and process emotions. If, for example, a child's parents are getting divorced, the child could easily begin believing that he did something wrong to cause the separation. The child could then believe that they are bad or wrong. This meaning made from the event then can carry over into adulthood, often at the subconscious or even unconscious level and engender feelings of insecurity, fear, and shame in everyday life.

As you can see, we can think of meaning making as a process of digestion. Events happen, feelings, thoughts, and sensations arise, and digesting the arising raw material then yields a product. What's left after this alchemical process is meaning. This meaning then gets written in our neural networks as memory. The more often we come to make the same meaning from arising situations, the stronger that neural pathway becomes, and the more likely it is that we make that meaning again and again.

The quintessential challenge of change, healing, and growth is shifting our original meanings to new, more compassionate, reasonable, and accurate portrayals of said events. In the above example, that could mean the adult seeing that his parents did not get divorced through some fault of his own but through a lack of connectivity that was happening in his parent's marriage. The updated meaning then allows the adult to feel the pain of the separation for what it is, deeply troubling to his younger child self rather than as deeply painful because he sees himself at fault.

Psychologically, it's very important to be upset over the true cause of upset instead of being upset at the inaccurate story that we told ourselves. When we can locate ourselves in the accurate pain, we can fully grieve and fully release that pain. This process leads us to take appropriate responsibility for our healing.

Brené Brown is one of the most accessible writers and researchers on the topics of shame, vulnerability, and wholeheartedness. Through her rising strong process (Brown, 2015), there is great emphasis on what she calls "The Rumble." The rumble is a process where you examine the deeper meanings you are ascribing to triggering experiences and look for ways that you have created an inaccurate and, perhaps, self-negating story around that experience. Her thesis is that rumbling with the stories we tell ourselves until we find a more wholehearted explanation gives us the opportunity to grow, develop, and heal. She describes the result of the rumbling as a true inner revolution.

Viktor Frankl writes extensively about the meaning making process in *Man's Search for Meaning* (2006). He writes

> *To be sure, man's search for meaning may arouse inner tension rather than inner equilibrium. However, precisely such tension is an indispensable prerequisite of mental health. There is nothing in the world, I venture to say, that would so effectively help one to survive even the worst conditions as the knowledge that there is a meaning in one's life. There is much wisdom in the words of Nietzsche: "He who has a why to live for can bear almost any how." (p. 103-04)*

Inevitably with the visionary plant medicine work, our experiences will offer opportunities to refashion our original stories as our deeply held insecurities and pain rise to the surface. It is highly important to work with an expert guide throughout the meaning-making process because often our own ideas of what certain visionary experiences mean can be incomplete. Through the support of expert guidance, reflection, time, and practice often the meanings we make of our visionary experiences shift and evolve.

It can be helpful to "try on" certain meanings to see if they fit. Through inner work and outer guidance, we see if the meaning fits or if it evolves or deepens in some way. What we are looking for in determining whether a meaning fits is a felt sense of resonance. Resonance in this case is defined as evoking a response. With time and consistent engagement, we will come to know the meaning that makes the most sense to our minds, hearts, and bodies – that which feels most true and invokes the most ease through time. All healing is a movement toward relaxation. When something is experienced as deeply true, it is deeply felt. Some feel it in their heart or gut, or in the body somewhere; others have a clear knowing that something is true.

When we come in contact with our personal truth and patterns, we are transformed. That transformation is a key part of the meaning-making process specifically and part of the healing process more widely. Finding our personal truth is like finding bedrock inside of ourselves. It feels solid and unshakable. We can rely and depend on it. From that bedrock we can build a more complete and compassionate self-conception that supports our growth and unfolding into an expression of our essential nature. When our meaning-making function in the integration process lands us in becoming more deeply self-aware and in creating personal truth, we also find ourselves in the realm of wisdom.

House (2007) notes psychedelic practitioners become more self-aware, particularly of patterns of personal defense mechanisms. Through this level of self-awareness, practitioners "were able to avail themselves to a level of inner wisdom not commonly accessible" (p. 178).

Merriam-Webster (n.d.) defines wisdom as "knowledge that is gained by having many experiences in life; the natural ability to understand things that most people don't understand; [and] knowledge of what is proper and reasonable: good sense or judgment" (n.p.). Merriam-Webster (n.d.) highlights that wisdom includes facets of insight, knowledge, and judgment.

Developing wisdom then aids us in all of our future meaning-making processes as we have greater insight, knowledge, and judgment. With the development of wisdom, we are much more likely to know what the inaccurate, self-disparaging stories are that we tell ourselves and become aware of them when they are bubbling up, and we are much less likely to believe those old stories and act out of them. With the development of wisdom, we have the ability to choose a new story, a new meaning, to live into.

Living into newer, more self-loving stories feels like freedom as the shackles from the past no longer tie us to patterns of unworthiness, shame, unlovability, isolation, and the like. It is my belief that the plants work to show us the places where we have created those meanings and are encouraging us to find ways to let them go, recreate them, and live into more authentic, grounded, and expansive expressions of ourselves and of Life.

CHAPTER 7

....

SPACIOUSNESS AND TIME

It's a gift; it's like there's a moment in which the thing is ready to let you see it. This comfortable, really deep way of getting a sense of something takes time. It doesn't show itself to you right away.

—Gary Snyder

Space often feels invisible although it is quite clear when it exists and when it does not! As we are working to change and become more fully ourselves, we need space to express that which is new. This means, quite simply, that we must release old ways and structures so there is space for what is healthier. Easier said than done however as old patterns, by definition, tend to want to stay on and continue to express themselves.

If we want to imagine spaciousness, we can visualize a beautiful bird flying through crests of mountaintops, soaring over valleys. We can remember times where we were sitting somewhere we experienced a wide expanse – an ocean, desert, a mountaintop, and the like.

Remember what you felt like in those spaces. Did you feel like you could breathe a little more easily? Open a little more widely? Imagine a different reality for yourself? Feel at peace?

In the midst of deep integration and healing, feeling this open possibility is terribly important (House, 2007). If we do not have space, how can we possibly change? How can we breathe ourselves into being more whole versions of ourselves? How can we imagine anything different than where we are now?

The visionary plant medicine experience offers a break from our day-to-day realities and thinking. It often opens up a space that was not there before, and, inside that space, much can be revealed (Walsh & Grob, 2007; House, 2007). That opportunity is wonderful, but it is not enough to fully integrate the changes that are necessary for us to grow into our whole selves. We need to keep opening up this spaciousness in our daily lives to make room for what wants to emerge.

Sometimes we are holding this space open for some time until the changes are made and integrated into our ways of being. A helpful way to think about this spaciousness would be to imagine the womb and the fertile space it offers new life to grow. Without the space created in the womb, no new life forms and is birthed.

We often do not know what is going to be created – what Spirit will want to birth next, but we can practice making the space available so that this can occur.

Space can look like many things in your life, and you will want to find the way to hold space for yourself. I often think that space holding involves openness, presence, lack of attachment to outcome, awareness of desires, commitment to the process, and reflection as well as comfort with the archetypal processes of dying, death, rebirth, and growth.

It can be a challenge to know how to hold space for yourself so it can also be helpful to work with someone who can hold space for you. This person can hold you in your essential self nature while you move into that expression of yourself. We often need others to "see" us before we can see ourselves in a new more whole way. It helps to have someone believe in us so we can receive positive support while we are making deep changes.

An important question to ask yourself is, "Do I have enough free space in my life to let my mind and heart roam?" If you answer yes to this question, you need to make space to integrate.

Spaciousness of mind means that you can create a time when you are not having to think about much for work or your personal life. The mind needs time to wander and drift, allowing the subconscious and unconscious space to emerge and speak. Time in nature or working on creative projects can be wonderful ways to free up mind space.

Spaciousness of the heart means taking time to relax so that emotions can surface and process through. Taking time to rest and breathe often makes space for the heart to open. Positive relationships can help relax the heart as well and create space for emotions to express themselves and move. The feeling of peace is of paramount importance for heart spaciousness. Letting the heart breathe does just that. If you have places, people, words, and/or things that help you access peacefulness, it's helpful to tap into those.

CHAPTER 8

....

NATURE AND GROUNDING

Those who contemplate the beauty of the earth find reserves of strength that will endure as long as life lasts.... There is something infinitely healing in the repeated refrains of nature — the assurance that dawn comes after night, and spring after winter."

—Rachel Carson

One touch of nature makes the whole world kin.

—William Shakespeare

Similar to many sections of this guidebook preceding this one, I cannot over emphasize the importance of connection to nature and grounding work to support integration. It's wonderful to fly, but at some point we all must land. Nature provides elemental support that is key for soothing frayed edges and instrumental in facilitating the deep releases, nourishment, quietness, and clarity that is necessary for the alchemical transformation of healing and integration to occur.

I've often felt that many are drawn to visionary plant medicine practice as a way to more deeply connect with Mother Nature. The plant teachers often initiate profound connections with the natural world and the cosmos, unfolding the hidden messages of Life. What better way to support this learning than to continue connecting with the earth, the sky, and the elementals outside of ceremony?

When I closed my ceremonial group facilitation with psilocybin mushrooms last year, I asked Spirit, "What next?" Spirit responded by telling me that I needed to teach elemental wisdom. What I mean by elemental wisdom are the understanding and teachings that can come from studying with the elements of earth, fire, water, and air, most basically. Earth-based traditions often contain other elements such as ether, mineral, and nature, to name a few. The elementals have great power and often predate the use of visionary plant medicine for healing and awakening. I felt like I was being called back to the roots of earth-based spirituality in order to help folks ground their ceremonial work much more solidly.

My work with Malidoma Patrice Some and Liv Wheeler, among others, gave me my initial foundation in elemental medicine so I began to draw upon that, intuiting what else was needed. In my home community of Miami, Florida, we worked with the elements over and over again in ceremony to invite the elemental wisdom and healing to come through. Over and over again, powerful healing experiences happened.

From earth we learned abundance, nourishment, presence, and grounding. We felt the strong foundation beneath our bodies and opened to being supported in a whole new way. We allowed ourselves to release pent up tension, trauma, and stress, falling into the reverie of the baby being held at the bosom. We gave our gratitude for our earth mother for all that she provides – our bodies, food, shelter, water, and beauty.

From water, we dove into the powerful feminine energy of cleansing, letting go, and flow. We allowed ourselves to be washed clean of all impurities, surrendering to that which is ready to be released. We immersed ourselves in the power of transformation and infinite flexibility water naturally possesses. We acknowledged the life that water creates and its power to support our emotional lives.

From air, we learned the power of breath and voice, cleansing, movement, subtle touch, the power of the invisible, and mental clarity. We felt the winds move through us, lightening our energetic loads and brushing us clean of unwanted detritus. We felt the movement of Spirit in the primordial *prana* and *qi*. As we breathed with intention, we allowed our minds to clear and communication to open at a deeper level.

From fire, we embraced the power of alchemy and transformation. We felt our human connection to the elementals as fire is the only element that humans can make. We felt the deep connection to Spirit in the constant changing and shifting plasma waves. We gave up what we were ready to release, letting it be burned through, sacrificed for our continued purification towards our most essential selves.

So there are very specific ritual practices that can be done to support your integration process by embracing the elements. The elements can be called on, invoked, prayed to, celebrated, and honored. The elements are teachers with much to share.

Even more basic perhaps than elemental work would be the practice of earthing. In his recent work, Ober, Sinatra, and Zucker (2010) describe the plethora of benefits of earthing, which can loosely be described as touching the soles of your feet to the earth for at least 20 minutes per day. A simple practice once a natural part of daily human life, has a variety of physical and mental health benefits. Perhaps most powerfully, earthing reduces inflammation and calms the nervous system. Many see chronic physical conditions begin to heal and levels of stress and anxiety lessen.

Even more basic than the practice of earthing would be allowing yourself to sit or walk in nature, becoming mindful of your surroundings and letting yourself absorb the richness of life. There are many spontaneous lessons of life that nature teaches. Putting yourself in nature allows life to teach you. We are life so what we learn in nature has direct parallels to our personal growth, healing, and integration.

As Satish Kumar (n.d.) so beautifully writes

> *When we view existence with such an expanded consciousness then it is possible to open our eyes and learn "from" nature rather than learn "about" nature. Nature is the greatest teacher. The Buddha learnt the reality of interdependence from a tree. While sitting under a tree and observing how everything was dependent upon everything else he was enlightened. Fruit came from flower, flower from branches, branches and leaves grow from the trunk, the trunk from the soil, the soil is nourished by the rain, the rain is held by the clouds, clouds are formed out of the sea, the sea receives the waters of the rivers and is held by the earth, the sea nourishes the earth and earth the sea and so it goes on. The Buddha's realisation of interdependence was perhaps the beginning of deep ecology and reverential ecology. (n.p.)*

Nature is perhaps our greatest teacher of integration. She cleanses and purges, continuing to build her harmonious web of life. Nature exemplifies simplicity, balance, spontaneity, and wholeness. By immersing yourself in nature, your whole being learns how to release, purify, fortify, root, and grow. There is no end to this transformation into wholeness.

Winkelman (2007) writes

Self-awareness and psychological integration is enhanced by this view of complex linkages among all aspects of the natural world, including humans and the personal self. Contact with nature enhances this view of interconnectedness with nature and its connections with the structure of memory and other aspects of cognition. Input from the environment has formed the structures of the neural networks of our memory, making the structures of the natural world fundamental to and isomorphic with the representations of vision and spatial perception. These connections are enhanced by the psychedelics, reinforcing the experience of the correctness of the perceptions that emerge from the unconscious structures of the world and brain into consciousness by virtue of their iconic similarity. In visionary experiences, these images have implicit coding of information retrieved from the unconscious and transferred to awareness. The access to natural world structures provides a basis for information not ordinarily available to consciousness, and may also produce a general heightened awareness by increasing access to various channels of physical information normally excluded because of habituation. Image-based natural world structures provide access to evolutionarily earlier structures of the brain and their learning and memory processes. The psychological focus of shamanic ritual and the physiological integrative effects of the psychointegrator effects of psychedelic medicines together produce powerful therapeutic effects by enhancing the expression of aspects of the unconscious (p. 149).

A SPECIAL NOTE ON GROUNDING

Visionary plant medicine practice is inherently ungrounding due to its destabilization of your normal waking consciousness. Especially with repeated and frequent use, many practitioners are ungrounded and unaware if it. Special attention needs to be paid to connecting with the earth specifically after ceremony to reground. Without that regrounding process, some become more prone to "spaceyness" of mind and lack sufficient presence in their bodies to receive critical information such as bodily sensations and awareness of surroundings. If one is not careful, this absence of embodiment can be dangerous as accidents can happen more easily and the like. We are not meant to float outside of our bodies or be partly in and partly out. We are meant to fully inhabit our physicality so we can receive important cues from our body/mind and intuition. Often our perspectives shift when we ground as well as we are receiving much more information from ourselves and our surroundings.

I often recommend a practice of laying belly down on the earth for 20 or 30 minutes (or more) to help reground into the body. I advise folks to call on the power of Earth Mother to help them land more fully in their physicality and bring themselves home. Often people find the practice deeply soothing and nourishing. I recommend it immediately following ceremony to reground and also cleanse any remaining impurities and non-native energies. Some medicine folks are skilled at cleansings, but some are not. Often folks go home with unwanted energies that can wreak havoc on wellbeing. For that reason, I recommend asking the earth to remove any impurities and energies that do not belong to you. This practice can be done as often as you like. As you develop your intuition more fully, you will know when you need this practice.

CHAPTER 9

....

ADEQUATE PHYSICAL CARE

The first wealth is health.

—Ralph Waldo Emerson

Walking is man's best medicine.

—Hippocrates

Integration is a total process. What I mean by that is that it requires a working through on all levels –- the physical especially. Providing your body with adequate physical support at the basic levels helps your system process what it needs to in an organic, natural way.

DIET, SUPPLEMENTATION, AND WATER

If your diet is taxing your physical body, it is not helping you integrate either. Common wisdom ensues. The healthiest diets are mostly plant-based, involve eating whole foods, and getting plenty of nutrients. Some folk's physical bodies do not tolerate a mostly raw diet, for instance, because the energy needed to digest raw foods can be substantial for a system that is already struggling. Others do quite well with a mostly raw diet and that is ideal for them. If you are called toward animal protein or fish, common sense these days says to look for grassfed, free-range, wild, and organic varieties so as to avoid toxins and environmentally-damaging meats.

Supplementation can be extremely necessary if vital nutrients are depleted. Most are experiencing some form of depletion nowadays with mineral and/or vitamin levels.

Also intensive visionary plant medicine work can be depleting as well as the body goes through a great level of intensity during the ceremonial experiences. Following the *dieta*, or the prescribed diet for visionary plant medicine work, is key to working with many plants and necessary to avoid physical harm as well. I advise you to follow a clean, whole foods, organic when possible diet following your visionary plant medicine work as well as before it.

A significant factor for health and wellbeing is the quality of your water. Most folks are not processing tap water and sometimes even filtered water with any great success. The best waters to drink in the United States are natural spring waters enclosed in glass containers. Mountain Valley Spring or Starky's are two companies that offer this as they are sourced from springs deep inside the earth. These waters are full of minerals and other nutrients necessary for the body's proper functioning. I personally struggled with reverse osmosis filtered water. My body was rejecting it because my body did not recognize it as it had been stripped of its vital minerals.

Without proper water, the body begins to be filled with toxins as waste cannot be adequately removed. The body also cannot properly digest foods and absorb nutrients without water. The body basically becomes dehydrated even if you are drinking a lot of water but not the right kind. It seems frustrating, but it's better to know this information rather than continue to deprive the body of what it most needs.

If your body cannot take in nourishment or release toxins, how will it ever be able to process through trauma and integrate deeply?

It can often take months to nourish your body properly depending on how depleted you are. Keep in mind that it could take at least 6 months to begin to help your body back into shape. I advise you to consult with a reputable alternative health care provider who is sensitive enough to know what supplements and foods best serve you where you are at this moment. Eating well, and nourishing yourself properly more generally, requires a deep, long term commitment.

And, the upside is huge.

EXERCISE AND MOVEMENT

Exercise and movement dovetail seamlessly with nutrition as primary supports for physical wellbeing. Energy needs to move in the body otherwise it gets stuck and can fester. As you move your body, energy moves through your body helping to push through whatever your body is trying to release. Exercise increases blood flow and brings more oxygen to your cells, both of which create positive physical states.

You will need to consider your state of fitness and wellbeing as you choose exercise and movement practices. It can be wonderful to mix several forms of movement to provide the body with different sorts of experiences to help it heal itself. More meditative exercises like Qi Gong, Tai Chi, and gentle forms of yoga can strengthen the energetic body as well as the physical one. More intensive forms of exercise that initiate sweating for the body can be quite cleansing. It is important to not overstress the body, however, as intensive exercise itself can be depleting if your body is not ready for it.

It's best to consult with a sensitive fitness practitioner or ask the alternative health care practitioner that you are working with for the nutritional support and forms of exercise that are most supportive. I advise you to find forms of movement that you enjoy as you will not practice other forms!

Walking, dancing, running, swimming, weight training, yoga, pilates, surfing, hiking, rock climbing, sailing, boxing, martial arts, and the like can all be wonderful. Find something you love!

REST

Perhaps this should go without saying, but in our steadily intensifying culture, high quality rest is often going by the wayside. After work with visionary plant medicine, much rest is needed. The body can naturally heal itself, but it needs the raw ingredients in order to do so. Rest is one of those raw ingredients. Taking naps, making extra space for sleeping in when possible, going to bed earlier, and choosing more restful activities like reading or listening to music all help. Our electronic diets often trick our bodies into thinking it's still daytime, so removing yourself from work at the computer 1-2 hours before going to sleep is critical so that your circadian rhythms are not disrupted and prevent you from resting deeply enough during the time you are asleep. Without enough deep sleep during the night, the body cannot repair itself adequately and becomes increasingly depleted and challenged.

The common wisdom after a visionary plant medicine ceremony is to not schedule yourself heavily for a few days afterwards. I would suggest that if you are committed to the integration process, you have to make space for rest as a permanent fixture in your life. As you are processing deeply held traumas or making profound changes, the body and mind will need space to rest and recharge itself.

A PERSONAL NOTE

During one of my ayahuasca ceremonies, the spirit of the plant told me that I should do whatever it takes to become healthy physically, mentally, emotionally, and spiritually. This was emphasized to be of profound importance for all of us. When we are healthy, we are able to be sovereign in ourselves. When we are not healthy, we are vulnerable to losing control of ourselves and being overly influenced by others. The warning was well taken, and I have been devoting myself to health even more so than before. I share this story with you from my personal experience to support the idea of you creating a deeper platform for your own health.

CHAPTER 10

CULTIVATING VIRTUES

In the end, only three things matter: how much you loved, how gently you lived, and how gracefully you let go of things not meant for you.

—Buddha

What if the journey of visionary plant medicine integration was about growing in spiritual maturity and cultivating quintessential human virtues? Virtues determine "the hows" of being and acting in the world. How do you approach yourself and others? How do you respond when you're stressed or compromised? How would you like to approach yourself and the world?

Ultimately, we are shaping ourselves through experiences, and, moving towards personal spiritual maturity, we are becoming more wholehearted and more capable of being humble, compassionate, strong, open, resilient, loving, responsible, discerning, courageous, persevering, honest, wise, just, patient, accepting, disciplined, and the like. As visionary plant medicine puts us in touch with the aspects of ourselves that need refining, we have the chance to cultivate some of these higher qualities of being that then open us to living as more pure expressions of our most essential selves.

Take for example the idea that San Pedro could show a person the ways that their heart remains closed – places where they have not been able to forgive themselves and others. San Pedro then shows a person what it feels like to open the heart completely and what it's like to experience the world free from relational pain and hurt. They experience the lightness, joy, and powerful level of communion that is possible from that place of overwhelming love.

As they return from that visionary plant medicine experience and work to integrate what they've seen and learned, the visionary plant medicine practitioner will want to begin addressing and resolving the past pains and hurts that keep their heart closed and/or fearful. Resolving past hurt often involves rooting out deeply embedded belief systems of unlovability and unworthiness as well. Letting those pains go and resolving them through the support of trusted others, experts or otherwise, then opens up the space for the heart to respond differently. From that newer, more open space, the person has the possibility of being more open, loving, compassionate, and accepting. Engaging in these virtuous behaviors begins to build new pathways of behavior that become easier and easier to enact and the cultivation of virtue continues as inspired by visionary plant medicine.

As many researchers and scholars of visionary medicines have stated, changing behavior towards being more positive, wholesome, and healthy is the gold standard for success (Goldsmith, 2007; House, 2007; Marsden & Lukoff; Stolaroff, 1993). Through the openings and awareness provided by visionary plant medicine, followed up by healing/therapeutic work, and through practicing new behaviors in spiritual practices and/or personal practices, the development of virtues is highly possible. Having a base for spiritual practice in an established spiritual tradition offers support for cultivating virtues as those virtues are already an integral part of established traditions.

Buddhism suggests that there are 10 main virtues, or *paramitas* (Mrozik, 2004). The 10 *paramitas* are *dana*, or generosity, *sila*, or morality, *upekkha*, or equanimity, *nekkhama*, or renunciation, *panna*, or wisdom, *viriya*, or effort, *khanti*, or forbearance, *sacca*, or truthfulness, *metta*, or loving-kindness, and *adhitthana*, or determination. Any practitioner of visionary plant medicine, for example, could consider these virtues as goals for their personal healing and integration.

Outside of formal religious tradition, Brené Brown (2010) offers a more secular set of 10 virtues to living wholeheartedly. As with any cultivation, the cultivation of virtues means changing one's behavior. Her 10 virtues are authenticity, self-compassion, resiliency of spirit, gratitude and joy, intuition and faith, creativity, play and rest, calm and stillness, meaningful work, and laughter, song, and dance (Brown, 2010). These 10 virtues then make up a guide to living wholeheartedly. She defines wholehearted living as "engaging in our lives from a place of worthiness" (p. 1) and notes that cultivating each of these virtues is a life-long practice.

CHAPTER 11

....

TURNING OUTWARD: THE RETURN TO THE WORLD

When you love with no conditions, you the human, and you the God, align with the Spirit of Life moving through you. Your life becomes the expression of the beauty of the Spirit. Life is nothing but a dream, and if you create your life with Love, your dream becomes a masterpiece of art.

—Don Miguel Ruiz

Mysticism is defined as the "experience of deep communion with ultimate reality as reported by mystics" (Merriam-Webster, n.p.). There are many who have acknowledged that deep mystical development often necessitates a withdrawal from the world in some way (Coder, 2011; Wapnick, 1980; Woods, 1996). The mystic withdrawal from the world prepares the aspirant for activity in the world after he or she returns (Woods, 1996). The worldly disengagement allows a mystic to presence "the most deeply ingrained ideals and aspirations of the society from which she has withdrawn in the process of disclosing the elements of her own mysterious call and destiny" (Woods, 1996, p. 162).

This time away allows a mystic to detach in a way that breaks down socially conditioned habitual behaviors and speeds up the individuation process, leading to personal transformation (Woods, 1996). Through this alchemical process, the mystic becomes more free and creative, more aware of dominant social norms, and capable of discerning reality as it is. The transformed aspirant can love more readily (Coder, 2011; Woods, 1996).

Woods (1996) writes, "All turning away is turning towards" (p. 165). The withdrawal and transformation necessarily lead to the final stage of mystical development, return.

> *What stimulates the mystic's return to society is not love alone. Rather, the mystic is drawn to the world from which she had withdrawn in order to carry back the answers to the questions—her society's questions, which she had borne within her into her solitude, and which were raised to consciousness in the process of reflection, assessment, and reintegration. Having recovered the integral vision of the society which produced her, the mystic must*

communicate that vision in word and deed. (Woods, 1996, p. 166)

We can begin to see that one of the main points of withdrawing from the world into deep spiritual, or mystic study, is to be able to return to the world with a more complete understanding of the world and a more developed sense of personhood that is capable of being in the world with a higher degree of consciousness. McGinn (2006) notes that mysticism is ultimately "meant to spill out and over into a new mode of living" (p. 519). As Wapnick (1980) showed, mystics' reintegration into the world was the "ultimate purpose of withdrawal" (p. 167). In Coder's (2011) study exemplar of spiritually advanced social change agency, Native American Mona Polacca shared that the teachings in the Native American Church mandate contemplation and social action. She explained further:

> *In my teachings one of the things that we say is [that]... , we're in that circle inside the tepee, and the altar is a half moon. That's the spirituality. That's the prayer, but when you walk out the door what you do and how you walk in your life is what makes the moon full.... The prayer and spirituality is important, but you also have to live life and put it into action. Put that prayer into action.*

Walsh (1989) showed these same insights in his writings on the psychology of human survival, stating that

> *psychological maturity is associated with a greater orientation toward service.... Since many of the causes of our crises stem from normative cultural beliefs and values, then the effectiveness of the people will depend on the cultural biases. This is the process of "detribalization," by which a person matures from an ethnocentric to a global worldview, develops "perspectivism" (the capacity to take other people's perspective).... Such a person no longer looks through, but rather looks at the cultural filters and hence can work on them. In short we need people of wisdom and maturity who not only work to relieve suffering, but also use their work for psychological growth, learning, and awakening of themselves and others. This process of "service-learning" as it is sometimes called is of course a form of the millennia-old tradition of karma yoga, the discipline in which service and work are viewed as opportunities for learning and awakening. The aim is impeccable service that optimally relieves suffering and awakens both self and others. In doing so, it aims at inclusive treatment of both symptom and cause, self and other, psyche and world. (p. 176)*

Goldsmith (2007) notes that "Every bodhisattva must return to society until all are liberated, and to derive full, healthful, integral benefit from psychedelic experiences, engagement in consensus reality must be seen as part of the good work of personal and societal development," (p. 123).

As Masters (2010) explains, "In turning toward our pain, we also, however indirectly, turn towards others' pain, both on the personal and collective level, (in both personal and collective contexts), and so our compassion for others deepens and widens" (p. 53).

As this guidebook has alluded to and stated outright at times, the crux of visionary plant medicine integration is how we move back into the world and participate. This guidebook has spoken specifically to intrapersonal development and how well one has healed underlying traumas and complexes, adopted healthier behavioral patterns, cultivated virtues, and, ultimately, developed spiritually so that access to greater personal freedom and essential nature is much more present. From this place of greater personal integration, one is much more capable of meeting the world of consensual reality powerfully.

Finding ways to be of service and turn your love outward can be highly rewarding, and is, perhaps, your responsibility as a more capable human being in this conflicted and paradoxical world. As your integration process evolves, consider what you'd like to offer the world. How can you be a greater expression of beauty, truth, and love? What does your essential self want to express as part of its unfolding?

APPENDIX

....

THEORETICAL BASIS AND SCIENTIFIC SUPPORT FOR VISIONARY PLANT MEDICINE INTEGRATION

The theory behind visionary plant medicine integration is nothing new to the Western scientific community that has studied it. The initial experimentation with mescaline, LSD, psilocybin, and MDMA by psychiatrists and researchers included time to process the psychedelic experiences with trained professionals (Goldsmith, 2007; Grob, 1994; House, 2007; Metzer, 1998; Passie, 2012; Naranjo, 1973; Stolaroff, 1993).

Starting in Switzerland in the late 1940s, low-doses of LSD were being used by psychiatrists with patients. They appeared to show a "release of repressed psychic material" (Grob, 1994, p. 4). This early work with psychedelic-assisted therapy was called "psycholytic," which means "soul-loosening" (Passie, 2012). Psycholytic therapy involved the use of low and medium doses of psychedelics to "activate psychological processes and make the unconscious material... accessible for psychotherapeutic processing" (Passie, 2012, p. 13). Psycholytic therapies were studied in both Europe and the United States and were seen to be particularly effective with patients who had "rigid defense mechanisms and excessively strict superego structures" (Grob, 1994, p. 4).

Distinctions came to be known in low-dose versus high-dose treatment approaches as well. The high-dose treatment approach seemed to yield an experience of an "entirely new and novel dimension of consciousness" (Grob, 1994, p. 5). In the 1950s, English psychiatrist Henry Osmond first explored this new high-dose paradigm in his studies of the treatment of alcoholism. He discovered that his successes were found mostly when subjects reached mystical and transcendent states of consciousness. In 1957, as a result of his work, Osmond introduced the term "psychedelic" as a way to account for the positive "enriching and life-changing" effects of these compounds. Between 1950 and 1965, some 40,000 patients were treated with LSD, and more than 1000 papers were written on the subject (Grob, 1994).

Current rigorous studies at Johns Hopkins University, New York University, Charleston Medical University of South Carolina, University of California Los Angeles (UCLA), University of Arizona, and through the support from organizations such as the Multidisciplinary Association for Psychedelic Studies (MAPS), the Beckley Foundation, and the Heffter Research Institute with psilocybin and MDMA conform to treatment protocols that include time for preparation and integration of the psychedelic experiences (Bouso et al., 2008; Garcia-Romeu, Griffiths, & Johnson, 2014; Griffiths et al., 2008; Grob et al., 2011; Guss, n.d.; MAPS, 1999; Mithoefer, 2013; Moreno et al., 2006). The meaning-making aspect of this process along with the assistance from professional guides has been shown to be integral to treatment success. Strassman (1997) explains that not integrating these powerful experiences can lead to a belief that things have shifted when, in fact, they have not, which can put the practitioner in a worse off place than before the visionary medicine experience.

Ralph Metzner, a veteran luminary in the field of psychedelic studies, describes that psychedelics have been proven to assist in healing presuming that both set and setting promoted confidence, ease, and safety on the part of the patient. In addition, presuming the conditions were supportive, patients can "gain therapeutic insight into neurotic and/or addictive emotional dynamics and behavior patterns and... can transcend fundamental self-concepts and views of the nature of reality" (Metzner, 1998).

In reporting on his pivotal study in the efficacy of enactogen-assisted psychotherapy treatment protocols, Passie (2012) highlights the importance of the work of integration:

Lasting benefit is much more likely achieved with follow-up therapy that aims to evaluate the experiences and integrate them into everyday life. In psycholytic therapy, the first concern is the feeling, viewing, and taking on that which was perceived, followed by its integration. It goes without saying that the newly won experiences, knowledge, and access to feelings have to be discussed and processed in a careful one-on-one session because this important work for integration cannot succeed if only done on one weekend packed with such intense experiences across several individuals. If this work is not individually processed, then that which was achieved may not be effectively anchored. (p. 65)

Mitheofer (2013) states

The challenges during the integration stage are to facilitate continued emotional processing and address any difficulties that arise as the experience from the session continues to unfold, and at the same time to help the participant apply the benefits gained in the MDMA-assisted sessions to daily life. These are likely to include valuable insights and perspectives, a broader emotional range and resilience, and deepened interpersonal skills. The therapists help the participant weave all aspects of the therapeutic experience into a new relationship with self, with others, and with her/his traumatic

> history. This phase of treatment brings these elements together in a cohesive, harmonious way.
>
> Since it is difficult to predict how much difficulty a given participant will have with the integration process, it is important to be alert to possible problems, such as shame and self-judgment about having revealed secrets, or challenging shifts in relationships and family systems as the participant heals and changes. Conversely, the therapists should be open to the possibility of an easy integration that requires minimal intervention beyond empathic listening and sharing appreciation for the participant's healing and growth. The therapists should therefore remain flexible in their response to each participant's particular needs. (p. 48)

Sean House (2007) conceptualizes a five-stage model for creating psychedelic-induced psychospiritual change that aligns beautifully with my own ideas of visionary plant medicine integration. In his model, the intention-setting process comes first, providing the foundation for the experience. Next the ingestion stage produces the altered state of consciousness and the specific effects of the substance. Insight is the third stage. As House (2007) writes, "When used with therapeutic intent these changes in perception often take the form of psychological insight.... Insight stems from paying attention to these phenomena and staying with the experience as it unfolds in its various manifestations" (p. 176). When insight is an intention, "psychological cleansing" (House, 2007, p. 177) can occur where a practitioner can self-reflect "without self-deception or illusion" (p. 177).

House (2007) defines integration as the "cognitive processes of meaning-making of the psychedelic experience and incorporating that meaning into one's perspectives on self and the world" (p. 179). He notes that integration begins during the psychedelic-induced altered state of consciousness (ASC) and can continue for days, weeks, months, and even years following. In some cases, integration can be completed within the ASC-based experience itself. However, often "the experience is either too confusing, too extensive, too powerful, or too metaphoric to be fully integrated" (House, 2007, p. 179). The ASC produces "Intense shifts of perception... [that can require] a good amount of dedicated integration work to rebalance the psychic frameworks that have been penetrated" (House, 2007, p. 179).

To promote healthy integration, House (2007) explains that the day after the session is best left open, free of other responsibilities so that the experience can be contemplated. Psychotherapeutic relationships can serve to "greatly enhance the integration process" (House, 2007, p. 180), especially as psychedelic experience can bring up conflicts with "deeply-held beliefs" (House, 2007, p. 180). Sometimes integration does not occur or can be very challenging for a variety of reasons. The experiences themselves can lend to difficulty processing information as thoughts are rapid, language is not readily available, and emotions can be tumultuous.

One of House's (2007) participants referred to challenges of integration, stating

> For me, in some ways the easiest part is to have extraordinary experiences. The hardest part is to integrate them.... They took me so far that I had to get beyond the confusion. There were times that the confusion became so overwhelming just even sensorially, that I thought I sunk into insanity from which there was no return. And I had to get through that somehow. So they're useful catalysts, but the experience that is ultimately beneficial needs to go beyond. The psychedelic won't produce that intrinsically. It will drop you over the edge into someplace where you have to struggle to get out. (p. 182)

The last phase of House's (2007) model is implementation. He describes his integration phase as cognitive and emotional and the last phase as behavioral. He describes implementation as "the gold standard of psychotherapeutic success" (House, 2007, p. 183), noting that it can require focused effort or happen more naturally.

> Implementing one's insights requires acting in ways that are congruent with what was learned. This involves psychotherapeutic and spiritual praxis following psychedelic sessions. Often this takes the form of engaging in new behaviors such as seeing

and appreciating spiritual manifestations in the world for the first time or actively overcoming one's psychological games. It may also mean increasing the frequency of already existing behaviors such as being more focused and productive in a certain area, acting more lovingly towards one's self or one's partner, or becoming more consistent in one's meditation practice. (House, 2007, p. 183)

Marsden and Lukoff (2007) define integration as "the explication of meaning of the experience and incorporating that meaning into one's conscious life" (p. 301). They note it can refer to short- or long-term process. An immediate form of integration can take place directly after the experience where the experience is remembered, processed, and analyzed. Feedback can be given and received. Marsden and Lukoff (2007) noted that this period is crucial for integration because much can be recalled about the experience itself and it helps participants move from the ASC to ordinary reality. In the next phase of integration, participants return to their homes, families, relationships, and work and apply the experiences. In their study, the authors note how the participants expressed responsibility for making the changes the psychedelic showed them was necessary.

REFERENCES

Bombaci, B. (2014, April 13). *Susto: Fright and soul loss in the Spanish speaking world.* Lulu Press. Retrieved September 16, 2016 from https://books.google.com/books?isbn=1312100567

Bombay, A., Matheson, K., & Anisman, H. (2009, November). Intergenerational trauma: Convergence of multiple processes among First Nations peoples in Canada. *Journal of Aboriginal Health, November 2009,* 6-47. Retrieved September 16, 2016 from http://www.naho.ca/documents/journal/ jaho5_03/05_03_01_Intergenerational.pdf

Bouso, J. C., Doblin, R., Farre, M., Alcazar, M. A., & Gomez-Jarabo, G. (2008). MDMA-Assisted psychotherapy using low doses in a small sample of women with chronic posttraumatic stress disorder. *Journal of Psychoactive Drugs, 40*(3), 225-236.

Brown, B. (2010). *The gifts of imperfection.* Center City, MN: Hazeldon.

Brown, B. (2012). *Daring greatly.* New York, NY: Avery.

Brown. B. (2015). *Rising strong.* London, UK: Vermilion.

Coder, K. E. (2011). "Shaking the world awake": An interfaith multiple case study of spiritually advanced social change agents. (Unpublished doctoral dissertation). Institute of Transpersonal Psychology, Palo Alto, CA.

Cook-Greuter, S. R. (1999). *Postautonomous ego development: A study of its nature and measurement.* Unpublished doctoral dissertation, Harvard University, Cambridge, MA.

Cook-Greuter, S. R. (2005). *Ego development: Nine levels of increasing embrace.* Retrieved March 6, 2007, from http://www.cook-greuter.com/

Cortright, B., Kahn, M., & Hess, J. (2003). Speaking from the heart: Integral T-groups as a tool for training transpersonal psychotherapists. *Journal of Transpersonal Psychology, 35*(2), 127-142.

Coyle, S. (2014). Intergenerational trauma – Legacies of loss. *Social Work Today, 14*(3), 18. Retrieved September 16, 2016 from http://www.socialworktoday.com/archive/051214p18.shtml

Daniels, M. (2013). Traditional roots, history, and evolution of the transpersonal perspective (pp. 23-43). In *The Wiley-Blackwell handbook of transpersonal psychology* (H. L. Friedman and G. Hartelius, Eds.). West Sussex, UK: Wiley Blackwell.

De Mori, B. B. (2014). From the native's point of view: How Shipibo-Konibo experience and interpret ayahuasca drinking with "gringos". In B. C. Labate and C. Canvar (Eds.), *Ayahuasca shamanism in the Amazon and beyond* (pp. 206-300). Oxford, UK: Oxford University Press.

ERIE. (n.d.). Integration Guidelines for Entheogenic Experiences. Entheogenic Research, Integration, and Education. Retrieved August 15, 2016 from https://www.erievision.org/integration-3

Firman, J., & Gila, A. (1997). *The primal wound: A transpersonal view of trauma, addiction, and growth.* Albany, NY: SUNY Press.

Frager, R., & Fadiman, J. (1984). *Personality and personal growth* (2nd ed.). New York, NY: Harper Collins.

Frankl, V. E. (2006). *Man's search for meaning.* Boston, MA: Beacon Press.

Fotiou, E. (2014). On the uneasiness of tourism: Considerations on shamanic tourism in Western Amazonia. In B. C. Labate and C. Canvar (Eds.), *Ayahuasca shamanism in the Amazon and beyond* (pp. 159-81). Oxford, UK: Oxford University Press.

Freedman, F. B. (2014). Shamans' networks in Western Amazonia. In B. C. Labate and C. Canvar (Eds.), *Ayahuasca shamanism in the Amazon and beyond* (pp. 130-58). Oxford, UK: Oxford University Press.

Garcia-Romeu, A., Griffiths, R, & Johnson, M. W. (2014). Psilocybin-occasioned mystical experiences in the treatment of tobacco addiction. *Current drug abuse reviews, 7*(3), 157-164.

Goldsmith, N. (2007). The ten lessons of psychedelic psychotherapy, rediscovered. In M. J. Winkelman and T. B. Roberts (Eds.), *Psychedelic medicine: New evidence for hal-*

lucinogenic substances as treatments (pp. 107-141). Westport, CT: Praeger.

Griffiths, R. R., Richards, W. A., Johnson, M.W., McCann, U. D., & Jesse, R. (2008). Mystical-type experiences occasioned by psilocybin mediate the attribution of personal meaning and spiritual significance 14 months later. *Journal of Psychopharmacology, 22*(6), 621–632.

Grob, C.S. (1994). Psychiatric research with hallucinogens: What have we learned? *Yearbook for Ethnomedicine and the Study of Consciousness, 3*, 1-10. Retrieved from http://www.druglibrary.org/schaffer/lsd/grob.htm

Grob, C. S., Danforth, A. L., Chopra, G. S., Hagerty, M., McKay, C. R., Halberstadt, A. L., Greer, G. R. (2011, January 3). Pilot study of psilocybin treatment for anxiety in patients with advanced-stage cancer. *Arch Gen Psychiatry, 68*(1), 71-78. doi:10.1001/archgenpsychiatry.2010.116.

Guss, J. (n.d.). Psilocybin Cancer Anxiety Research Project's Psychedelic Psychotherapy Training Program. MAPS Co-Sponsored Courses. Retrieved September 30, 2016 from http://www.spiritualcompetency.com /mapsQuiz.aspx?courseID=49

Harvey, A. (2009). *The hope: A guide to sacred activism.* New York, NY: Hay House.

Hollis, J. (2005). *Finding meaning in the second half of life: How to finally, really grow up.* New York, NY: Gotham Books.

House, S. G. (2007). Common processes in psychedelic-induced psychospiritual change. In M. J. Winkelman and T. B. Roberts (Eds.), *Psychedelic medicine: New evidence for hallucinogenic substances as treatments* (pp. 169-93). Westport, CT: Praeger.

Karen, R. (1998). *Becoming attached: First relationships and how they shape our capacity to love.* Oxford, UK: Oxford University Press.

Kegan, R. (1994). *In over our heads: The mental demands of modern life.* Cambridge, MA: Harvard University Press.

Kumar, S. (n.d.) Learning from nature. In Resurgence & Ecologist. Retrieved September 5, 2016 from http://www.resurgence.org/satish-kumar/articles/learning-from-nature.html

Labate, B. C., & Cavnar, C. (2014). *Ayahuasca shamanism in the Amazon and beyond.* Oxford, UK: Oxford University Press.

Labate, B. C., Cavnar, C., & Freedman, F. B. (2014). Notes on the expansion and reinvention of ayahuasca shamanism. In B. C. Labate and C. Canvar (Eds.), *Ayahuasca shamanism in the Amazon and beyond* (pp. 3-15). Oxford, UK: Oxford University Press.

Landgon, E. J., & De Rose, I. S. (2014). Medicine alliance: Contemporary shamanic networks in Brazil. In B. C. Labate and C. Canvar (Eds.), *Ayahuasca shamanism in the Amazon and beyond* (pp. 81-104). Oxford, UK: Oxford University Press.

Levine, P. (1997). *Waking the tiger: Healing trauma.* Berkeley, CA: North Atlantic Books.

Losonczy, A. M., & Cappo, S. M. (2014). Ritualized misunderstanding between uncertainty, agreement, and rupture: Communication patterns in Euro-American ayahuasca ritual interactions. In B. C. Labate and C. Canvar (Eds.), *Ayahuasca shamanism in the Amazon and beyond* (pp. 105-29). Oxford, UK: Oxford University Press.

Luskin, F. (2004). Transformative practices for integrating mind-body-spirit. *The Journal of Alternative and Complementary Medicine, 10*(1), S-15-S-23.

MacDonald, D. A., Walsh, R., & Shapiro, S. L. (2013). Meditation: Empirical research and future directions. In H. L. Friedman and G. Hartelius (Eds.), *The Wiley-Blackwell handbook of transpersonal psychology* (pp. 433-458). West Sussex, UK: Wiley Blackwell.

MAPS (1999, Spring). *From the Bulletin of the Multidisciplinary Association of Psychedelic Studies, 9*(1), 24-29.

Marsden, R. & Lukoff, D. (2007). Transpersonal healing with hallucinogens. In M. J. Winkelman and T. B. Roberts (Eds.), *Psychedelic medicine: New evidence for hallucinogenic substances as treatments* (pp. 287-305). Westport, CT: Praeger.

Masters, R. A. (2010). *Spiritual bypassing: When spirituality disconnects us from what really matters*. Berkeley, CA: North Atlantic Books.

McGinn, B. (Ed.). (2006). *The essential writings of Christian mysticism*. New York, NY: The Modern Library.

McKenna, T. (1992). *Food of the gods: The search for the original tree of knowledge.* New York, NY: Bantam Books.

Metzner, R. (1998). Hallucinogenic drugs and plants in psychotherapy and shamanism. *Journal of Psychoactive Drugs, 30*(4), 1-10.

Merriam-Webster (n.d.). Mysticism. Retrieved March 6, 2017 from http://www.merriam-webster.com/dictionary/mysticism

Merriam-Webster (n.d.). Wisdom. Retrieved September 5, 2016 from http://www.merriam-webster.com/dictionary/wisdom

Mithoefer, M., et al. (2011, November). *A manual for MDMA-assisted psychotherapy in the treatment of posttraumatic stress disorder.* Santa Cruz, CA: MAPS.

Mithoefer, M. C., Wagner, M. T., et al. (2011). The safety and efficacy of {+/-} 3,4- methylenedioxymethamphetamine-assisted psychotherapy in subjects with chronic, treatment-resistant posttraumatic stress disorder: The first randomized controlled pilot study. *Journal of Psychopharmacology, 25*(4), 439-452.

Moreno, F. A., Wiegand, C. B., Taitano, E. K., & Delgado, P. L. (2006). Safety, tolerability, and efficacy of psilocybin in 9 patients with Obsessive-Compulsive Disorder. *Journal of Clinical Psychiatry, 67*(11), 1635-1740.

Mrozik, S. (2004). Cooking living beings: The transformative effects of encounters with bodhisattva bodies.

Journal of Religious Ethics, 32(1), 175-194. Retrieved from http://www.wiley.com/bw/journal.asp?ref=0384-9694

Naranjo, C. (1973). *The healing journey: New approaches to consciousness.* New York, NY: Ballantine Books.

Ober, C., Sinatra, S.T., & Zucker, M. (2010). *Earthing: The most important health discovery ever?* Laguna Beach, CA: Basic Health Publications.

Passie. T. (2012). *Healing with enactogens: Therapist and patient perspectives on MDMA-assisted group psychotherapy.* Santa Cruz, CA: Multidisciplinary Association for Psychedelic Studies.

Portney, C. (2003, April 1). Intergenerational transmission of trauma: An introduction for the clinician. *Psychiatric Times.* Retrieved September 16, 2016 from http://www.psychiatrictimes.com/articles/intergenerational-transmission-trauma-introduction-clinician

Razvi, S. (2016, October 7). Trauma dynamics and MDMA workshop [PowerPoint Presentation]. University of Denver.

Rocha, T. (2014, June 25). The Dark Knight of the Souls. *The Atlantic.* Retrieved from https://www.theatlantic.com/health/archive/2014/06/the-dark-knight-of-the-souls/372766/

Saez, O. C. (2014). Authentic ayahuasca. In B. C. Labate and C. Canvar (Eds.), *Ayahuasca shamanism in the Amazon and beyond* (pp. xix-xxv). Oxford, UK: Oxford University Press.

Sayin, H. U. (2014). The consumption of psychoactive plants during religious rituals: The roots of common symbols and figures in religions and myths. *Neuro-Quantology, 12*(2), 276-296.

Schlitz, M., Vieten, C., & Amorok, T. (2007). *Living deeply: The art and science of transformation in everyday life.* Oakland, CA: New Harbinger.

Shepard, G. H. (2014). Will the real shaman please stand up? The recent adoption of ayahuasca among indigenous groups of the Peruvian Amazon. In B. C. Labate and C. Canvar (Eds.), *Ayahuasca shamanism in the Amazon and beyond* (pp. 16-39). Oxford, UK: Oxford University Press.

Siegel, D. J. (2001). Toward an interpersonal neurobiology of the developing mind: Attachment relationships, "mindsight," and neural integration. *Infant Mental Health Journal, 22*(1-2), 67-94.

Siegel, D. J. (2007). An interpersonal neurobiology of psychotherapy: The developing mind and the resolution of trauma. In M. F. Solomon and D. J. Siegel (Eds.), *Healing trauma: Attachment, mind, body, and brain* (pp. 1-56). New York, NY: W. W. Norton.

Siegel, D. J. (2007). *The mindful brain: Reflection and attunement in the cultivation of well-being.* New York, NY: W. W. Norton.

Stolaroff, M. (1993). Using psychedelics wisely. *Gnosis, 26,* 1-6.

Strassman, R. J. (1997). Biomedical research with psychedelics; Current models and future prospects. In *Etheogens and the future of religion* (R. Fortne, Ed.). (pp. 153-62). San Francisco, CA: Council on Spiritual Practices.

Virtanen, P. K. (2014). Materializing alliances: Ayahuasca shamanism in and beyond Western Amazonian indigenous communities. In B. C. Labate and C. Canvar (Eds.), *Ayahuasca shamanism in the Amazon and beyond* (pp. 59-80). Oxford, UK: Oxford University Press.

Wall. K., Nye, F., & FitzMedrud, E. (2013). Psychospiritual integrative practices. In H. L. Friedman and G. Hartelius (Eds.), *The Wiley-Blackwell handbook of transpersonal psychology* (pp. 544-561). West Sussex, UK: Wiley Blackwell.

Wallin, D. J. (2007). *Attachment in psychotherapy.* New York, NY: The Guilford Press.

Walsh, R. (1989). Toward a psychology of human survival: Psychological approaches to contemporary global threats. *American Journal of Psychotherapy, 43*(2), 158-180. Retrieved from http://www.ajp.org/

Walsh, R., & Grob, C. S. (2007). Psychological health and growth. In M. J. Winkelman and T. B. Roberts (Eds.), *Psychedelic medicine: New evidence for hallucinogenic substances as treatments* (pp. 213-25). Westport, CT: Praeger.

Wapnick, K. (1980). Mysticism and schizophrenia. *Journal of Transpersonal Psychology, 1*(2), 49-67. Retrieved from http://www.atpweb.org/journal.aspx

Watts, A. W. (2013/1962). *The joyous cosmology: Adventures in the chemistry of consciousness* (2nd ed.). Novato, CA: New World Library.

Wilber, K. (1993). Paths beyond ego in the coming decade. In R. Walsh & F. Vaughan (Eds.), *Paths beyond ego: The transpersonal vision* (pp. 256-266). New York, NY: Jeremy P. Tarcher/Putnam.

Wilber, K. (2001). The evolution of consciousness. In *A brief history of everything* (2nd ed., pp. 125-142). Boston, MA: Shambhala.

Wilber, K. (2006). *Integral spirituality.* Boston, MA: Integral Books.

Wilber, K. (2007). *The integral vision: A very short introduction to the revolutionary integral approach to life, God, the universe, and everything.* Boston, MA: Shambhala.

Winkelman (2007). Shamanic guidelines for psychedelic medicine. In M. J. Winkelman and T. B. Roberts (Eds.), *Psychedelic medicine: New evidence for hallucinogenic substances as treatments* (pp. 143-67). Westport, CT: Praeger.

Woods, R. (1996). Mysticism and social action: The mystic's calling development, and social activity. *Journal of Consciousness Studies, 3*(2), 158-171. Retrieved from http:// www.imprint.co.uk/jcs.html

RECOMMENDED READING

Brown, B. (2012). *Daring greatly.* New York, NY: Avery.

Brown. B. (2015). *Rising strong.* London, UK: Vermilion.

ERIE. (n.d.). Integration Guidelines for Entheogenic Experiences. Entheogenic Research, Integration, and Education. Retrieved August 15, 2016 from https://www.erievision.org/integration-3

Hollis, J. (2005). *Finding meaning in the second half of life: How to finally, really grow up.* New York, NY: Gotham Books.

Goldsmith, N. (2007). The ten lessons of psychedelic psychotherapy, rediscovered. In M. J. Winkelman and T. B. Roberts (Eds.), *Psychedelic medicine: New evidence for hallucinogenic substances as treatments* (pp. 107-141). Westport, CT: Praeger.

Labate, B. C., & Cavnar, C. (2014). *Ayahuasca shamanism in the Amazon and beyond.* Oxford, UK: Oxford University Press.

Masters, R. A. (2010). *Spiritual bypassing: When spirituality disconnects us from what really matters.* Berkeley, CA: North Atlantic Books.

Ober, C., Sinatra, S.T., & Zucker, M. (2010). *Earthing: The most important health discovery ever?* Laguna Beach, CA: Basic Health Publications.

Watts, A. W. (2013/1962). *The joyous cosmology: Adventures in the chemistry of consciousness* (2nd ed.). Novato, CA: New World Library.

ABOUT THE AUTHOR

Katherine Coder, PhD is a Transpersonal Psychologist, guide, and teacher. She works through elemental medicine, one-on-one meetings, and group trainings and ceremonies. Katherine invites people to realize and express their full humanness – to themselves, in relationship, and in community. Her specialties include trauma resolution, visionary plant medicine integration work, deep feminine cultivation, ceremony, and individual client work. Her transformative work connects body, mind, and Spirit to allow people to integrate at a profound level and live from true essence. She is the cofounder of the Sacred Elemental Wisdom Institute, a community practice that educates women in elemental medicine and ceremony.

Katherine comes to her specialization of visionary plant medicine integration work through her studies in transpersonal psychology, her own personal exploration of visionary plant practice for healing, and her service as a visionary plant medicine guide. Along her path, she worked with ayahuasca, psilocybin mushrooms, kambo, huachuma, tobacco, and iboga through medicine holders from Colombia, Ecuador, Gabon, and Peru among other places. After her ceremonies with iboga, she felt that she had found the early trauma that her deeper self was searching for, and she began to bring her visionary plant work to a close and started down the long road of integration. She currently practices complete sobriety from all substance use, including alcohol, and supports others through the process of integration.

She can be reached through her website at www.katherinecoder.com, her Facebook page Katherine Coder, PhD or by email to drkat@katherinecoder.com. She can also be reached through the Sacred Elemental Wisdom community at www.sacredelementalwisdom.org.

Join the Visionary Plant Medicine Integration tribe on Facebook @vpmintegration. If you would like to work privately, please email Katherine directly.

www.ingramcontent.com/pod-product-compliance
Lightning Source LLC
Chambersburg PA
CBHW070627300426
44113CB00010B/1693